THE JOHNSON METHOD
GUIDEBOOK FOR NEW TRACTOR-TRAILER DRIVERS

TERRENCE JOHNSON
Class A Commercial Vehicle "Safe Driver" License
Clean Background & Driving History
Certified New Driver Mentor

Johnson Craftworks LLC
All rights reserved © 2023
United States of America

The Johnson Method
Guidebook For New Tractor-Trailer Drivers

Copyright © 2023
Terrence Johnson
United States of America

All rights reserved. No part of this guidebook may be copied, reproduced, recorded, photocopied, transmitted, or distributed in any form or by any means. The only exceptions are in the case of an approved written request of permitted use from the author, and brief quotations used in reviews.

To send a request for permitted use, contact the author. Contact information is located in the last pages of this guidebook. Request a permitted use form, fill the form with your information and return to the author. You will be contacted with approval or denial of permitted use.

Cover art and book design by Terrence Johnson.

ISBNs
eBook: 979-8-9877194-0-4
Paperback: 979-8-9877194-1-1

Published by:
Johnson Craftworks LLC

OFFICIAL LEGAL DISCLAIMER

All information, recommendations, and procedures in this guidebook are not designed to replace your following of DOT laws and regulations. They are not designed to replace the directions given by law enforcement, DOT officers, security officers, shipping clerks, and truck company staff. They are not designed to replace or substitute the training, information, and instruction given by any school, instructor, or CDL manual. They are not designed to change any DOT laws, regulations, or school training.

Always follow the road rules and laws as designed in the locations you drive, wherever you drive. Always follow the road signs and the direction of any legally authorized persons who direct traffic. Always follow construction signs and devices to prevent incidents and collisions. Wear your seat belt whenever the key is in the ignition, whether the engine (or power) is on or not. Always drive safely.

Johnson Craftworks LLC is owned by Terrence Johnson. Johnson Craftworks LLC, and its owner are not liable for any person or entity who misuse the information, recommendations, and procedures within this guidebook. Johnson Craftworks LLC and its owner are not liable for any person who use the information, recommendations, and procedures in this guidebook to break any law, damage any equipment, and damage any property.

Johnson Craftworks LLC and its owner are not liable for any person or entity who use the information, recommendations, and procedures in this guidebook to cause any kind of harm (physically, emotionally, verbally, ext.) to any other person, animal, or entity, including themselves.

The names of particular truck stops, students, truck companies, and persons will not be revealed in this guidebook. They have a right to privacy of their identity. Any truck stops, person of any kind, and examples are only used as examples, and not provided to degrade or pedestal any person's or company's reputation.

The information, recommendations, and procedures in this guidebook are not designed to degrade or pedestal the reputation, legality, debt, or profit of any business, contract, law, regulation, agreement, exchange, person, entity, or organization. Johnson Craftworks LLC and its owner are not liable for the degradation or pedestaling of any business, contract, law, regulation, agreement, exchange, person, entity, or organization.

ABOUT AUTHOR

My name is Terrence, but you can call me Mr. J or sir!

It happens every so often. I will be driving, or one of my students will be driving, and I see a very familiar scene. It takes me back to the dreams I had as a boy. In those dreams, I drove big rigs on various roads. Oh yes! I knew one day I was going to be a truck driver! It was just a matter of time... and of course legal age and a valid Commercial Driver License! Ha!

HOW IT ALL STARTED

I remember the excitement of receiving my Learner's License when I was 16 years of age. When I turned 17 years of age, I obtained my Class E Driver License. Immediately I found myself driving everything, from cars, to vans, exotic cars, modified cars, and even 26' U-Haul trucks when I turned 18.

It was common for people to ask me (a six-foot-tall young man) to help them move furniture. Who wouldn't ask? Over the years, I went on to become an automotive detailer, basic auto service technician, worked at a few furniture moving companies, and owned an LLC at one point moving furniture and other large/heavy items. In 2018 I earned my Class B CDL and drove Over The Road interstate for the first time.

I had a predisposition to Class A combination vehicles. I always thought I could still make good money and enjoy driving even with Class B trucks and didn't have to deal with the hassle of driving tractor-trailers. In 2018 I had my first glimpse of the trucking industry in a Class B straight truck. It wasn't as bad as I thought!

A NEW BEGINNING

But in late 2021, I found myself applying for a particular trucking company. I had fallen on hard times through no fault of my own and was redirected onto a new path. I took the opportunity even though I still had a predisposition to tractor-trailers.

    I enrolled in a 4-week trucking school. After I passed all the tests with ease, I moved out of Florida and on to Alabama so I could get picked up by a Driver Mentor from the company. Those two weeks driving a company tractor-trailer with the Driver Mentor onboard turned out to be a lot of fun. I mostly enjoyed that long drive to California and got to see some life-changing sights.

    Before I knew it, I was assigned a company tractor to drive, a brand new one at that. It was a 2023 and only had seven miles on the digital odometer. It was actually the very tractor I've always wanted to drive if I could buy my own tractor, a Peterbilt 579 sleeper cab. I named the truck, Lorena. It's a funny story, I'll explain later! I got my first dispatch and that was the beginning of it all.

    I drove solo and learned a great deal. One day I noticed a message on the ELD about the benefits of being a Driver Mentor (or New Driver Trainer as I say) for the company. I called the company and asked for more details, and they mentioned that they could run me through the checks and balances to see if I would qualify. I heard back from them not long after and was qualified to be a Driver Mentor!

LEADING THE WAY FORWARD

It wasn't any difficult for me. I was a manager at a job when I was in my early twenties, owned an LLC before, and usually became a team leader at other jobs I worked. I enjoyed being a Driver Mentor. I train all my students thoroughly and brought them up to a minimal (but high) standard of driving ability and safety. My students and I have plenty of fun though; we share our life experiences, see many amazing sights across America, eat great food at various restaurants, laugh a lot, and of course do a lot of driving. I love me some truck drivin'!

Driving tractor-trailers is more than just driving, it's an experience, a life-changing one at that. Upon first meeting the students, we introduce ourselves, they put their stuff in the truck (they sit in the passenger seat), and then I drive for the first three days before they get into the hot seat. I usually tell them some funny stories of mine to ease any tension or anxiety they may have. After the third day, they are in the hot seat, and their real learning begins.

THE TRUTH REVEALED

While driving for this particular company, as well as being a Driver Mentor, I realized some wonderful and some not so wonderful things about the trucking industry, as well as issues with training new drivers. This would spark the interest of writing this very guidebook. It is very common to hear "I want to start my own truck company." Another good one is: "If I buy some trucks and hire drivers, I will make a fortune and could retire early." At one point, I desired to do the same.

But the issue I found is that the industry has a high turnover rate, there is difficulty with new drivers making the transition from driving a car to a large, heavy commercial vehicle. The issue is due to poor schooling, a lack of teaching certain very important things, holding onto bad driving habits from driving cars, and not being given all the information and tools they need upfront to be the safest, most professional, and timely drivers, before they go out to drive on their own.

I decided to write this guidebook to give important information to those who are interested in driving tractor-trailers, those who are in or have just left trucking school and need the 'other stuff' they don't teach, and finally to drivers who have been driving for a while but simply are interested in some new ways of performing their job that will create a safer industry and higher income.

From all that I have experienced while driving big rigs, training new drivers, and all the other job and life experience mixed in, I developed a very high standard for myself. I did everything I possibly could to be the safest driver, to deliver my loads in a timely manner, be courteous (and generous) to everyone I meet, and to perform the physical (and soft-skill) aspects of the job as efficiently as possible. It did well for me in every way! My desired outcome is to raise the bar and set higher standards for other drivers and the trucking industry as a whole. This guidebook will do it!

I know I won't drive or be a New Driver Trainer forever, so my desired result is that this guidebook help millions of people (and the trucking industry) even after I step out of the hot seat of life. I have personally (and literally) authored this guidebook for your benefit!

We will begin light and easy (appetizers sure are delicious!) with some simple but very necessary topics. After, we will work our way toward the meat and potatoes (or the bread and butter) of truck driving. This is The Johnson Method. Enjoy!

INTRODUCTION

This is a guidebook. It hold valuable information, recommendations, and procedures that will aid in your tractor-trailer driving experience.

Whether you are a company driver, owner-operator, or even an instructor, you will have to be in the hot seat to perform your job. The hot seat is not just the driver's seat. The hot seat is a position of control, self-judgement, challenge, and most definitely responsibility. You are not JUST a truck driver or instructor. Your job will affect billions of people's lives all across the Earth, not only on the highway you are driving, or the lot you train your students.

It is of utmost importance that you always drive and perform your job in a way that is safe, timely, courteous, generous, communicative, and professional. At no place, time, or circumstance should you engage in any behavior that is illegal, unsafe, or cause of conflict to others or yourself.

This guidebook is filled with the 'other stuff' that is not taught in trucking schools, and even some things that are not found in any CDL manual. The 'other stuff' is actually very necessary for your job. Most companies will have a Driver Trainer, or company staff whose responsibility is to provide some of the 'other stuff' to you in some form before you drive.

This is not always the case. But it is very common for Driver Trainers and company staff to not provide a thorough training of the 'other stuff'. It is not uncommon that new drivers are then given a company truck to drive and sent out while not being fully informed or having certain important tools they will need.

In this guidebook, I will also share some new technology that may soon come to the trucking industry. There may come a time when landing gear won't need to be raised and lowered using a crank handle. There may come a time where diesel fuel no longer need to be purchased or added to any tanks. There may be an additional line to hook/unhook (for a total of four) with respect to electric trailers and CEVs (Commercial Electric Vehicle).

Backing a tractor-trailer without a collision has been a thing of mystery for most people. It also remain a common area of trouble for many drivers, and even the most common cause of tractor-trailer collisions. Backing a tractor-trailer in general is not the same as a vehicle with no trailer attached. As I say, backing – is not JUST a maneuver, but the ultimate challenge of your driving skill.

We will take a look at the three most important backing maneuvers (plus two other maneuvers) I think every tractor-trailer driver need to know how to perform, and perform in a way that is safe, consistent, timely, smooth, without collision, and of course enjoyable. The methods of backing I will share with you will likely be different than it is taught in driving schools (if they are taught at all, seriously).

Call-to-actions are important. Anyone can talk. Anyone can say they can do something. But to actually do it, and do it in a safe, timely, and consistent manner without causing conflict or trouble…not everyone can DO that. They say money talks, but the only way you'll be able to make that money JUMP into your bank account as a tractor-trailer driver is by your performance. And your performance need to be up to a high standard.

LEGAL DISCLAIMER: "The procedures given in this guidebook should ONLY be performed with permission from your Driver Manager and company, and only in a way that is safe, does not break any laws, does not cause any kind of collision, and does not cause any harm or conflict with any person (including yourself). It is not recommended you perform anything shared in this guidebook at any truck driving school unless it is part of their training curriculum, and the instructors specifically instruct you to do so. While taking your CDL test, always follow the instructions given by the test giver. Always follow the rules and instructions of your driving school and instructors. The author and Johnson Craftworks LLC relinquish liability."

No, Lorena is not my girlfriend or wife! It is the name I gave to the truck the particular company assigned me to drive. It was just a question that popped in my head – "I wonder what I should name this truck?" Immediately after, just happened to look over and see a sign that said "Lorena Rd". Later, I looked up the meaning of that name, and it means 'victory'. Perfect! A name that I shared with my students and was a common cause of laughter by personifying the truck. Just remember, if you see the name Lorena mentioned anywhere in this guidebook, it is not in reference to any of my students, or any other woman.

It's known that most people would never consider driving a flatbed truck, even many truck drivers. There are specific reasons why, which I will not get into in this guidebook. But one thing for sure, there is one flatbed worth mentioning.

One of my students had a dream they were driving, Lorena being in the right lane, and a black flatbed tractor-trailer came beside us and somehow the flatbed lost control and rammed the side of Lorena. He said in the dream, we were pushed off the road and ended up crashing. But who would have known that in real life, he would see the exact black flatbed tractor-trailer drive beside him, on the same interstate he saw in the dream!

Luckily, the black flatbed tractor-trailer did not run us off the road, and drove on by as all the other trucks and cars do. It was a very interesting and spiritual event. Now, "There's that flatbed!" has been a token of good luck every time me or any of my students see one.

Every time we see a black flatbed tractor-trailer, we always say "There's that flatbed!" It serves a reminder that any of us could lose our lives at any time, and for any cause. But because what could have happened (according to that dream), did not happen, we know that if there is a such thing as a Divine Lord or God, we had our lives spared on that day.

So, if you ever see a black flatbed tractor-trailer, it is a good luck charm. It is a reminder that we should be more aware and thankful that we are privileged with another day of life. Thank your flatbed tractor-trailer drivers and the big rigs they drive for representing that! And also, for helping to transport the resources and materials that's needed to build and maintain this world we live in!

This is The Johnson Method! So, let's get to those appetizers!

LIST OF CONTENTS

The Faces of the Trucking Industry --------------------------------- 1

Trucking School -- 13

HIRED: The Onboarding Process ------------------------------------ 21

The Big Rig -- 25

Hours of Service --- 31

ELD Macros --- 43

The 5TH Wheel -- 47

Hook & Drop Trailers --- 51

Sliding Tandems -- 61

Maximum Weight Limits -- 65

Tractor-Trailers: Driving Forward -------------------------------- 71

Backing Maneuvers: The Pentaplex --------------------------------- 79

Trailer Load & Unload -- 91

Mountain Driving --- 95

The Bread & Butter -- 101

The Trucker Courtesy -- 113

Advanced Trucking Technology ------------------------------------ 117

Commercial Electric Vehicles (CEVs) ----------------------------- 119

Industry Changes -- 121

Conclusion -- 125

ACKNOWLEDGEMENTS -- 127

REVIEW THIS BOOK -- 129

BUY ME A COFFEE --- 131

PRODUCT STORE --- 135

SOCIAL MEDIA & CONTACT INFO ----------------------------------- 137
OTHER BOOKS BY AUTHOR --- 139

SECTION ONE
The Faces of the Trucking Industry

Life is all about people. But it is also true that people have needs, whether they be food, shelter, safer roads to travel, hygiene care products, or tools to allow them to perform daily activities faster and easier. It does take more than one person, actually hundreds of millions of people to extract, transport, manufacture, package, ship, and deliver these essential resources.

Because so many people are required for the complex logistical process of moving essential goods, there is a necessity for timely, efficient, and accurate usage of soft-skills. Whether you are verbally communicating, using the ELD, a hands-free device, hand signals, vehicle lights, scanning tools, or computers, it is part of everyone's job. Let's take a look at the soft-skills that will be useful for you, and all the people involved (in some way) in the trucking industry you will engage.

SOFT-SKILLS

Teamwork is absolutely necessary in your day-to-day job duties as a tractor-trailer driver. You will work with various kinds of people, and they all will have their own job duties. It is vital you are able to get along with everyone you encounter. They are all a significant part of the resource logistical system. Therefore, when you engage with others while on the job, remember that you are there to help make their job a little easier and smooth, as much as they are there to make yours as well.

Communication (or a lack of) is a very common issue amongst people that can mature into greater problems. It is not only the numbers and load information that need to be communicated, but also potential dangers and even smaller issues that may not seem important.

Always communicate clearly what you need, why you are where you are, and whether there is any additional information that others may need. What may seem insignificant to you might be very important for others to know. Never be afraid to ask questions, or relay information that you think or feel might impact your safety or job duties (or the safety or job duties of others).

It does not matter what profession, job, or industry you work, there are going to be some number of problems, and those problems can have varying levels of severity. The trucking industry is no stranger to problems and conflict. Problem solving is part of any and all jobs, no matter what you do. Even when everything seem to be going smoothly, still you never want to let your guard down. Always be alert, and always be ready to work alongside others through communication, should problems arise.

Critical thinking might not be something you would think is necessary being a tractor-trailer driver. "All you are doing is driving, driving is easy!" Oh, how wrong could that be! Even driving small passenger vehicles require critical thinking. At a moment's notice, anything could happen or change, and all of a sudden you could find yourself in the midst of danger or a possible collision.

Driving a tractor-trailer complicate this further, by the vehicle's size being larger, weight being heavier, and the pivoting of a tractor-trailer while backing and turning. It is necessary to not just drive, but to drive with open eyes that see, a free conscious that is alert, and a mind that is timely and efficient at processing information around you. This does mean to never drive when there is alcohol in your body, never drive while sleepy, and never drive while suffering from health issues of any kind that may impact your ability to utilize critical thinking behind the wheel.

People just don't have needs. They want their needs met when they want them, sometimes as soon as possible, and occasionally NOW. Time management is required to be a tractor-trailer driver. You will be dispatched to pick up and deliver loads, and those loads have time restrictions. Your Driver Manager will dispatch you on loads that each have their own delivery deadline, or a window of time in which the load will need to arrive at the designated location.

Teamwork, communication, critical thinking, and problem solving definitely help to get loads delivered on time. This will kindly reflect in less tension and conflict amongst industry workers, and higher paychecks along with fewer incidents and collisions.

As a tractor-trailer driver, especially if you will drive interstate, adaptability will be part of the job. You will constantly find yourself on roads you have never driven, around people who you have never met, situations which have their own complexities, and locations that will test your driving and backing skills. It will reward you with a constant supply of 'newness' and excitement as long as you are able to continually adapt, wherever you go, whatever you are doing, and whoever you engage with.

We will close out this chapter with a short description of each kind of person you will eventually engage with, while being a tractor-trailer driver, depending on your duties and specific load types.

RAW MATERIALISTS (FARMERS, MINERS, EXT.)

Everything we use has to come from raw substance. Raw substance has to be grown, captured, or pulled from the environment. From these raw substances, we can get a processed and more refined working material to use for making the products we need.

LANDOWNERS

All the buildings, homes, parks, roads, and landscapes we see are not just there, but they are all in some kind of asset market. Land is usually owned by companies, businesses, organizations, and people. They also may be listed for sale. Land is needed to extract the materials we need, to shelter and even process the materials as well. Landowners play an important role in the industry. There has to be physical places to perform the duties of moving goods from location to location.

CONSTRUCTION EQUIPMENT OPERATORS

Try digging up a field of salt with only your hand and packaging it out to millions of companies, processing facilities, and people. You will find yourself overwhelmed by the high demand and your inability to move the salt to keep up. So, construction equipment are designed to make the process of extracting raw material in a way that is faster, easier, safer, and more cost effective.

INSURANCE AGENTS

Land, buildings, equipment, vehicles, tools, and property all need insurance, in case of fire, vandalism, theft, and other risks. Insurance agents and companies provide protection and issuance of assets for businesses, owners, and other persons.

INVESTORS AND CONTRACTORS

Not everyone is privileged with big muscles, a useful invention idea, or the desire to work as an employee. There are those who have money and are good on a business level. So, they can take that money and business mind and use them to help get more people into the industry, or to help businesses get off the ground and expand. Investors and contractors help to fill in the grey areas, and function like buoyancy, which help to raise the industry off the ground so that more things can be moved and moved in a faster, safer, and more cost-effective manner.

INVENTORS

All the products you see on the shelf at your local stores and businesses once started out as an idea. Ideas are non-physical in nature, but when mixed with a plan, action, and physical material, now things which be not, become things which be. Powerful and deep minds are necessary to supply those ideas. They are the real foundation next to raw physical substances.

TRUCK DRIVERS

Imagine how quickly the world would turn upside down and end up in severe scarcity if all the truck drivers quit their jobs, or simply disappeared. There would be no one to transport the raw material to make (and transport again) the essentials we all use and need on a daily basis.

Store shelves would remain empty, construction projects would come to a halt, houses no longer built, auto production would stop, grocery stores would run completely out of food, fuel stations no longer with gasoline and diesel to fill your tanks with, personal hygiene products eventually would run out, ext. Truck drivers move the things we need and use. They are essential in this world and make up a large part of the resource logistical system.

MATERIAL PROCESSING FACILITY WORKERS

Not all raw material can be extracted from the environment and packaged while it is raw. Most raw material has to go through some amount of processing, whether it is to remove impurities, reduce size, separate what is needed from the parts that are not, or more complex processing methods. These facilities are built specifically to receive the raw material and process the material into something that is easier to mix with other substances, or package right away to be sold in the consumer market. The facility workers help to keep the facilities operational, clean, safe, and legal.

SHIPPERS & RECEIVERS

Once the raw material has been processed at least enough to be packaged (or palletized) and sold on the consumer market, shippers & receivers take care of the majority of the post-processing work. Shippers and receivers will carefully quantify, separate, mix, and package certain materials and products so they can be transported (by truck drivers) to businesses, people, land, other shippers, and receivers.

MANUFACTURERS

Once raw material has been processed at least enough to be packaged and sold on the consumer market, manufacturers take the post-processed material and create products that can be shelved at stores for consumers to purchase. Processing plants work raw materials into usable materials, and manufacturers work usable materials into products, and lastly consumers use products for their daily needs.

FORKLIFT OPERATORS

Once raw material is processed, it can be palletized to aid in the transportation of goods faster, easier, and more cost effective. Forklift operators move the palletized goods in and out of trailers, and around warehouses for organization.

PACKAGE HANDLERS

Not all material or products are handled through machines or are palletized. Sometimes materials and products need to be moved and organized manually by hand. Package handlers take the conscious role of doing just that.

STATE/FEDERAL INSPECTORS

Processing plants, warehouses, storage area, and other facilities require special inspection services to ensure safety, cleanliness, and adherence to certain laws and regulations.

STOCKERS

Once products are ready to be shelved, stockers move those products off trucks and into the stores for consumers to pick and purchase.

TRUCK FLEET OWNERS AND STAFF

At one point in time, truck companies were actually very few. There were a small handful of big names that controlled the entire market. But in the modern-day trucking world, truck companies are many and easy to be found. Trucks can't be purchased by anyone, and not anyone can own a truck fleet company. There is an entire process to opening a trucking company that is legal and meet the transportation industry standards. Truck fleet owners and staff create the trucking jobs that many apply for. They purchase, employ, and maintain the big rigs so that there are physically trucks and drivers to perform the duties of transporting goods.

TRUCK SCHOOL INSTRUCTORS

There are federal, state, and even company requirements that must be met before a person can obtain a Commercial Driver License and employed as a professional tractor-trailer driver. Truck schools take care of a big portion of the work as far as training students for the completion of a CDL exam and qualifications for employment by a truck company. These school instructors also must meet certain qualifications and requirements. They are responsible for providing the verbal, written, and hands-on instruction to their students.

NEW DRIVER TRAINERS

Sometimes called Mentors or Driver Mentors, New Driver Trainers work for truck companies and their duty is to train newly licensed drivers directly in the field. They will usually take students Over The Road and provide training of specific and necessary job duties.

DISPATCHERS AND LOAD PLANNERS

How are you going to find loads to transport? There are various systems and boards which hold the information of each load that is added to them. Load planners will look for loads for drivers, depending on their location, amount of driving time on their clock, and the kind of loads they can legally drive. Dispatchers work more direct with drivers. They not only dispatch the drivers on loads provided by the load planners, but dispatchers also function as driver managers. They will aid in the day-to-day duties and problems of the drivers they oversee. Some truck companies have the dispatcher and load planner as the same person.

SECURITY OFFICERS

People need goods. Unfortunately, this does require that goods be documented, secured, and protected while going through the storage, processing, and transportation process from theft, vandalism, and other illegal activities. Security officers work various rolls in the industry, from surveillance monitoring, documenting important information, enforcing company (federal and state laws as well) policies, and patrolling grounds (truck stops, processing facilities, shipper locations, truck lots, ext.).

DOT OFFICERS

Tractor-trailer drivers are human. They are not free from making mistakes, breaking laws, engaging in illegal behavior, and performing their duties in an unsafe manner. DOT Officers specialize in keeping the roads safe to drive and the vehicles we operate up to industry standards. They will perform DOT Inspections on tractors and trailers, run driver licenses for validity, check logs for violations, operate weigh stations, check permit books for validity, run speed traps, and various other operations.

LAW ENFORCEMENT

Along with DOT Officers, law enforcement also play an important role in keeping the roads safe, and vehicles operated up to industry standards. Don't be surprised if you get pulled over by police if you are speeding in a tractor-trailer, fail to use your turn signal while changing lanes, or drive down the road with your load unsecured.

THE FORCES

Drivers are also needed to transport vehicles and equipment for the Military, Air Force, and Army. Imagine having to move a tank cross-country or transport 200,000 weapons without the use of trucks and truck drivers.

PARAMEDICS AND FIREMEN

Wasn't it mentioned earlier that the trucking industry isn't free of problems? Collisions, incidents, fatalities, and health risks can and do happen. Thankfully, when they do happen, firemen (and firewomen) and paramedics come to the rescue. They are very important to the trucking industry.

COURT OFFICIALS

Lawsuits do happen in the trucking industry. And how are you going to pay that ticket you got? Courts handle the legal matters. Gone are the days of arming it out when two people are in a disagreement or a law is broken.

YARD DOGS

Most shippers, receivers, and manufactures will have hostler units and yard dogs (hostler drivers) to move trailers on the company premises. This prevent the need to have a big rig to move trailers. Hostlers are smaller, lighter, and make moving trailers a faster process. This save time money, and allows shippers, receivers, and manufacturers to operate more efficiently. They also help truck drivers to save time and money by not having to wait for their trailer to get unloaded or loaded. Yard dogs can also dock trailers to be loaded or unloaded so when the truck driver arrive, their load or empty trailer is ready to take immediately.

DIESEL REPAIR TECHNICIANS

Big rigs are not indestructible. They can and do break down and suffer from wear and tear. Diesel repair technicians fill in that need. They keep big rigs running well, and on the road. Big rigs are not entirely built like regular vehicles, and so specially trained technicians must work on them to ensure they remain up to mechanical standard, according to DOT laws, and up to industry standards.

MOBILE DIESEL TECHNICIANS

Big rigs can and do break down nowhere near a diesel repair facility. Depending on the kind and severity of the problem, mobile diesel repair technicians will drive to the location of the big rig to repair it on the scene.

TRUCKER PETS

Furry friends keep many truck drivers company while out driving for hours at a time, and away from home days or weeks at a time. Furry friends eliminate loneliness and provide companionship.

MARKETING AGENTS

Truck sales, advertisements for trucking jobs, ext. are the job of marketers and sales agents. Someone has to send out the information in front of the eyes of those who are potential buyers and applicants.

TRUCK STOP STAFF

Staff at truck stops ring up food and merchandise, clean the facilities, move product into stores for sales, and greet those who enter their stores with great customer service. They also take care of any issues involving fueling or cash advances initiated at the fuel pumps (charge stations for electric trucks, known as CEVs).

RIDESHARE, RENTAL CAR, HOTEL, BUS, AND AIRPORT STAFF

During the schooling, hiring, and even on duty process, you may have to get a rental car, stay at a hotel, catch a rideshare, or even a flight. It's not only products and materials that need to go from one location to another, but also people.

DINING AND RESTAURANT STAFF

You can work as hard as you want, eventually you will get hungry. There are plenty of restaurants and food stores (even at truck stops) to keep you with the energy you need to perform your day-to-day duties. Your family cook isn't the only one who will put food in your belly in your lifetime. There are plenty who will prepare, cook, and serve your meals while you are away from home.

JANITORS

Good food and cool merchandise are nothing if the facility you go to is filthy. Janitors are still commonly overlooked and underrated in our modern world. But imagine if they all quit their jobs or simply disappeared. You wouldn't want to walk foot in any store unless it was a life-or-death situation!

YOU

We can't forget about the MVP of the industry! That is, you! Truck drivers are the livelihood of our modern-day world, especially in the West. You deserve to feel proud of the dangerous, exhausting, and lengthy duty you perform to make sure homes get built, roads are paved, store shelves stocked with food and hygiene products, clothes are shipped to apparel stores, and so much more!

SECTION TWO
Trucking School

I remember first going to trucking school. Both my car and pickup truck broke down days before and the cost of fixing them was more than I could afford. They were older model vehicles anyway, so I decided to junk them and take cash. I ended up getting a scooter to ride to school every day. I didn't know what to expect, but truck school turned out to be a lot of fun. I learned more than I thought I would and met some interesting people. Fortunately, I passed the school and all the exams, and earned a Class A Commercial Driver License!

TRUCK SCHOOL INSTRUCTORS

There are federal and state requirements that must be met before a person can obtain a Class A Commercial Driver License. There are also requirements that must be met to be employed as a tractor-trailer driver at a truck company. Truck schools take care of a big portion of the work as far as training students for the completion of a CDL exam and qualifications for employment by a truck company.

The school instructors also must meet certain qualifications and requirements. They are responsible for providing the verbal, written, and hands-on instruction to their students.

They will train to the best of their ability. Some may be hard on you, others may be a little more relaxed and give you more seat time to practice. Follow the directions of your instructors, they have a difficult job, but still want to see you do well.

You will need to read and understand the state CDL manual of the state you wish to test in. If you are applying for employment at a particular truck company, it is wise to know if the company will pay for the license and schooling. If they do, you will need to study your state's CDL manual, and the company will schedule a date and time for you to test at a local DMV to obtain a Class A Commercial Learner's License.

If not, you will still need to read and understand your state's CDL manual and test at a local DMV to obtain a Class A Commercial Learner's License before you start trucking school. Either way, you must have successfully passed the necessary exams at a local DMV and obtained a Class A Commercial Learner's License before you can begin trucking school.

ENROLLED: IT'S CLASS TIME!

Each trucking school may teach different backing maneuvers. They will have different instructors, and each instructor will have their own (but reasonably similar) way of teaching pre-trip inspections and backing maneuvers.

You will certainly learn to pre-trip a tractor and trailer, which will also require an inside cab inspection and air brakes tests (for those testing for air brakes). For CEVs, testing of the power and electronic brakes will replace testing of air brakes, unless the CEV you operate has an electrically powered air compressor. Know what kind of truck you will operate, and whether it has air brakes or electronic brakes.

I find trucking schools do a well job teaching the pre-trip inspection. Backing maneuvers usually consist of straight-line back, offset backing, alley dock, and/or parallel parking.

I have heard of schools which don't teach alley dock (whether legal or not) and I think that is a set up for failure! The alley dock is the bread and butter for tractor-trailer drivers. Even if you will never accept loads that require docking the trailer, you may still have to back and drop trailers in designated parking spaces.

Some truck schools also teach the 45 back, which is backing a tractor-trailer starting at a 45-degree angle from the parking space. Although the 45 back is not included in the list of maneuvers I feel is important for all truck drivers to know, we will still take a look at it in chapter 12 - "BACKING MANEUVERS: THE PENTAPLEX". It may come in handy for you.

THE GREAT CHALLENGE FOR TRUCKING SCHOOLS

I am never surprised when I hear of a tractor-trailer collision or incident, regardless if it was from backing, while making a turn, or on the interstate. This is even more so if the driver was a new driver. While training my students, and while interacting with other drivers and new drivers, I have become aware of a very alarming issue. See, driving a tractor-trailer (especially backing) is not the same as a car and non-pivoting vehicle.

The very fact that tractor-trailers pivot, and have long, oversized trailers, create a very steep learning curve for new tractor-trailer drivers. It is not primarily an issue with safety or poor instruction from trucking schools. The weight, size, gearing, and design of tractor-trailers do not match what most people have driven all of their lives. The vehicles are completely different, but the habits and abilities of the driver, if not readjusted, create a mismatch. This translates into a new driver maneuvering a tractor-trailer as they do small, non-pivoting vehicles.

New drivers just aren't aware how different driving a tractor-trailer is compared to a car and non-pivoting vehicle. Some truck school instructors and company trainers also have difficulty (or simply don't) help new tractor-trailer drivers make the readjustment and transition.

Think about it; most people who have driven all of their lives, have mostly driven smaller cars and trucks, not oversized, overweight pivoting vehicles with short gearing, long wheelbases, and wide turning radiuses with long trailers hooked. They have spent years and even decades developing habits and abilities that match small, non-pivoting vehicles, and not of tractor-trailers.

This pose many problems, such as not adjusting their driving to match the weight, size, length, and pivoting of a tractor-trailer. This result in common issues such as: not turning wide and hitting curbs or objects on the inside of the turn, too little following distance behind other vehicles, braking too late and too hard while approaching stop signs and red lights, and turning early and not being able to complete forward maneuvers without hitting objects due to trailer off-tracking.

More issues include: making turns at too high a speed, riding the foot brake going down hills and mountains (trucks speed up on downgrades), not looking far ahead to account for the long braking distance of tractor-tailers in the event of an emergency stop, backing only using mirrors (and not getting out to look), and not using engine/exhaust brakes while descending long and steep downgrades.

I have to iron out each of those 'car driving' habits from each of my students, and make adjustments to their driving to account for the weight, size, length, gearing, and pivoting of a tractor-trailer. The difference is night and day. It is interesting to see them improve their driving according to the tractor-trailer.

They smile when they realize that they CAN drive a tractor-trailer without a collision or feeling like they will lose control of the truck. Making the adjustment is necessary. It will reduce collisions, incidents, and truly improve safety. Truck school instructors and company mentors work specifically to help new tractor-trailer drivers make those adjustments, but it isn't as easy as it sound.

TRUCKS: TRAINING FEMALE STUDENTS

I remember being confused when I heard on television one day that there weren't any women in truck driving, and there was a push to get women into trucking. All my life I have met plenty of female truck drivers who had been driving for 10, 20, and even 30 plus years. And even now I do. I saw that as dishonoring to all the women truck drivers that have always been in the industry.

I later learned though, that really what was happening was a push to bring MORE women into the trucking industry due to an often mentioned 'driver shortage' that seem to never go away. So, bringing more women into the trucking industry was a move to eliminate or at least suppress the 'driver shortage' issue.

There has never been a DRIVER shortage in the trucking industry, but there surely has been a high turnover rate for various reasons. Plenty of the population have a CDL, and many at one point worked in, or attempted to work in the trucking industry. But due to issues which have remained in the trucking industry for a very long time, many of them bailed while in process or stayed for a short time before leaving, for various reasons.

Training women for driving a tractor-trailer is certainly different than with men. Other drivers, school instructors, and company mentors would agree. I personally have found that women students (not all) can be anxious, nervous, and sometimes feel 'lost' due to being emotionally overwhelmed by the size and complexity of a tractor-trailer alone. Then factor in the complete difference in driving required to not cause a collision or lose control, and it is easy to become overwhelmed, emotionally speaking.

Training women students has not been difficult for me, because for the same reasons, I initially never wanted to drive tractor-trailers. I figured a 26' box truck was more than enough, and I'd make a good living off just that. How wrong could I have been! I actually enjoy driving tractor-trailers more than box trucks now, and all those fears and anxieties were just inner issues that had nothing to do with trucks or driving.

WOMEN CAN DO IT TOO

What seem to work, is helping women students to relax, and training them one step at a time. Even better is to allow them to work through their emotions first, before pushing them to back a truck or get on the road. Sometimes we just aren't comfortable yet when it comes to new things that are overwhelming. No woman wants to fail or cause a problem; that's an emotional burden, which is painful and undesirable. But if a woman is in trucking school, she has enough confidence to face her fears. She is there for a reason.

So, I train women students to have a different frame of thinking, or feeling I should say, that driving a tractor-trailer is an ENJOYABLE experience and nothing to be afraid of, something that will be rewarding for them. They are simply just getting comfortable, emotionally speaking.

I remember the first time one of my women students alley docked with no pullups, and performed it smoothly and in a timely manner, without the truck being crooked or hitting anything, and she had a BIG grin on her face. See, it can be done! Face your fears, they are the gatekeepers to greater joy and success!

THE NEXT STEP

After you have passed trucking school and earned a Class A Commercial Driver License, next is time to get employed. If you have applied to drive for a particular truck company, they will lead you the rest of the way. If you have attended trucking school on your own, you will need to apply and qualify for a driving position at a truck company.

SECTION THREE
HIRED: The Onboarding Process

Applying for (and being employed by) a truck company as a tractor-trailer driver might be different than other jobs. You aren't going to just drive a few miles down the road, fill out a paper application, wait a day or two for an interview (to find out if you got the job or not), and when you begin working.

You will go through a thorough screening process. Requirements are: valid Class A Commercial Driver License, background check, driving record check, drug test, work history, and a medical examination specific for commercial vehicle drivers. You will be required to have completed a full course at a truck school.

Some companies will also have you take an online course before they onboard you. Paperwork such as direct deposit, medical benefits, tax forms, and others may need to be completed and sent to the company before they onboard you.

If you meet the requirements, you will then need to arrive at one of their terminals. If you live close to one of their terminals or willing to drive there, that is an option. But always contact the company and ask if that is possible and if there would be any issues. If you are not close to one of their terminals, the company will either fly, rent a car, or bus you there. Other truck companies will send a driver mentor in a company truck to pick you up.

Depending on the time of arrival, you may need to get a hotel. Contact the company beforehand and know whether they will set up and pay for a hotel and for how long. In order to reduce expenses, some companies may have two onboarding drivers per room. If you must have a room by yourself for whatever reason, contact the company and know beforehand whether you will have the room to yourself, or whether you can get a room for only you.

Other companies may send a Mentor or Driver Trainer in a company truck to your location to pick you up. The Mentor or Driver Trainer will then provide Over The Road training. Each company has their own requirements for how long you will be on the truck with the Mentor and how many days or hours you will need to drive.

Also understand that the mentor does not have to let you continue to drive. For example, if you cause a collision, or drive carelessly, the company may not allow you to continue the onboarding process. Drive safely and follow the company's polices and mentor's directions. Always follow the road laws and instructions given from any DOT or law enforcement officer.

ORIENTATION

After you have made it to the terminal or pass the on the road training with the Mentor, you will begin orientation and may also be required to perform a tested backing maneuver, pre-trip inspection, and/or city driving. Next, you will be assigned a truck and Dispatcher or Driver Manager. The truck you are assigned could be a new truck or a used truck with miles. The truck may or may not be up to your cleanliness standards.

Truck companies save money by reusing trucks, rather than buying a new truck each time they need to assign a truck to a new driver. Truck companies usually clean and detail used trucks before assigning them to the next driver. If you must have a clean truck, your options would be to contact the company and ask for one, or you can bring your own cleaning supplies and clean the truck before placing your personal items and driving for your first load.

The onboarding process could take a week or a few weeks, and you may want to have some home time after all is finished. Usually, truck companies will get you a load to pick up that is headed toward where you live so you can have some home time. Speak with your Driver Manager or Dispatcher with regard to home time.

Congratulations! You are now an employed tractor-trailer driver! Your learning continues from here, and plenty of life-changing experiences!

SECTION FOUR
The Big Rig

You will need to perform a pre-trip inspection on whatever tractor is assigned to you. That first pre-trip inspection is so important. Never drive a tractor you have not visually and physically inspected. If there is anything missing, damaged, malfunctioned, or out of date on the tractor, it will need to be serviced before you drive. The worst-case scenario is that you may get reassigned to a different tractor.

TRUCK SET UP

You will be in the hot seat. Set up the tractor so you are comfortable while driving and have everything you need while out on the road. If you will be driving a day cab tractor, bring the absolute minimal you need for the day. A cluttered cab is difficult to move around in and can become uncomfortable or an eye-sore.

If you will be driving a sleeper cab tractor, you are able to bring more items with you. If you will be gone for days or weeks at a time, don't forget to bring bedding and a pillow. You'll need enough extra clothing for the time away from home. Abide by your company's policy with regard to what items they do and do not allow on their trucks.

Note: Possession of alcohol in a commercial vehicle is against the law, regardless of what company you work for.

Ensure the 5th wheel of the tractor is in an appropriate location, and it is properly greased. For more information on the 5th wheel, read chapter 7 – "The 5th Wheel". If the air connections and electrical line (including power line for electric trailers) are dangling with no or minimal support, it is wise to secure the airlines and electrical line, so they do not catch on something or drag on the catwalk. It may be necessary to zip-tie the lines so that they remain organized and close together.

RECOMMENDED ITEMS TO PURCHASE OR BRING

- Bedding, pillow, and blanket
- Phone dash mount
- 12v AUX charger (that has USB ports)
- Phone charging cable for your phone
- Wireless headset for hands-free operation
- Reflective vest (needed to enter premises of some shippers)
- Hard hat
- Clear, protective goggles
- Mini cutters (to cut metal seals)
- tire beater
- flashlight
- sunglasses
- work gloves
- clipboard
- writing pen
- stapler
- utility knife
- zip-ties
- extra glad hand seals

THE TRUCK THAT COULD NOT

Commercial motor vehicles (and CEVs) are not necessarily indestructible. You'll easily find trucks inside diesel repair shops getting fixed. Any company you drive for will want all of their drivers to take good care of the equipment. It saves the company money on repairs and keeps trucks on the road, meaning more profit can be made. Do you want higher paychecks? Take care of the truck. The trucks won't make you or the company any profit if it is sitting in the repair shop!

An easy way to keep trucks on the road is to always ensure the engine oil level is in the specified range. A low oil level can be disastrous for a diesel engine. A lack of oil and oil pressure cause excessive friction. Excessive friction cause high heat, wear, and tear. During the hot summer months, using a heavy diesel oil such as 15w-40 may help to keep oil from getting too hot and burning off. During cold winters, especially up North, a light diesel oil such as 10w-30 can help the oil from thickening when it is very cold out.

LEGAL DISCLAIMER: "Always use the oil as recommended by your company's policy and the tractor's factory manual. Using the wrong type and viscosity of oil can damage the engine. The author and Johnson Craftworks LLC relinquish liability."

Check the engine coolant level frequently, especially in extreme hot or cold conditions. The coolant level can suddenly decrease after turning the engine off for a few hours after driving, especially if the weather is very hot or cold. Keep the coolant level between the 'minimum' and 'maximum' lines, and according to the tractor's factory recommendations listed in its manual.

Imagine if the serpentine belt came off. You would lose power steering, air pressure, oil pressure, and engine cooling capabilities. It is important you check the engine's serpentine belt regularly.

The most sensitive parts of the truck are the 5th wheel and front suspension. Be cautious to avoid hitting potholes in the road, curbs, debris, and other things that may puncture the front tires or cause damage to the steering and suspension system. Be cautious to not ram the tractor into the trailer while hooking. Get the 5th wheel under the trailer, park, and then get out to make sure there is no space between the bottom of the trailer and the 5th wheel.

All you need to do is HOOK to the trailer with a gentle bump. There is no need to be aggressive while hooking to a trailer or reverse at a high speed. Be cautious to not ram the trailer to the dock when docking to get loaded, unloaded, or to dock drop a trailer. All you need is a gentle bump so that the trailer is up against the dock.

Most truck companies will have diesel shops at their terminals for basic maintenance, which includes airing the tires. Some truck stops also have air supply at one of their fuel isles if the tractor-trailer you are driving is low on air in one or more of the tires. Instructions for airing at truck stops are provided by the facility.

LEGAL DISCLAIMER: "Never attempt to add air to the tires. Always call someone or the truck stop staff and ask for assistance. The author and Johnson Craftworks LLC relinquish liability."

TRUCK WASH

The company you drive for may or may not have a truck wash facility on site. You may be required to wash the tractor and/or trailer elsewhere. Each company will have their own requirements. If your company does not require truck washing and it is a driver expense, you may have to use an outside truck wash service. Some truck wash facilities only perform trailer washouts for reefers. Others may only wash the outside of tractors and trailers and special locations will perform both services.

Truck washes are located everywhere. You may have to use a commercial truck specific navigation device or phone application to find them. Personally, I think a clean truck not only looks better, but show your professionalism and represent the company you work for in a positive way. Usually since I only drive drop & hook, I will just get the tractor itself washed since I am constantly switching trailers. If I were to stick with a single trailer, then I would wash both.

NOT YOUR TRUCK BUT STILL YOUR RESPONSIBILITY

Just because you are driving a company tractor-trailer does not mean you don't have to take care of it. Remember, that truck is what will make the company profit in order to pay you your wages. You also need to drive responsibly and safely to prevent collisions and fatalities.

Upgrades and modifications are common amongst big rigs, but it might be against your company's policy to modify or upgrade the truck in any way. Always ask your Driver Manager if and what modifications are legal and abide by company policy.

Common modifications amongst big rigs include neon lights in the interior and exterior of the tractor, exhaust stacks, metal lug nut caps, fog lights on the front bottom of the bumper, flatscreen TV installation in the sleeper area, and CB radios installed in the cab.

ANNUAL TRACTOR AND TRAILER INSPECTIONS

Every tractor and trailer must be inspected by a certified inspector annually. If you assigned to told to drive a tractor, you must review all of the documents in the permit book (registration, insurance, ext.) that they are up to date and legal. You must also look for the DOT inspection sticker or label on the outside of the truck and ensure that the inspection has been performed within the last 11 months. NEVER drive a tractor that has not been inspected within the last 11 months, or missing the documents in the permit book. Even if the documents are present in the permit book but they are out of date, you still are not legally able to drive that tractor.

The same is true for trailers. All trailers must be inspected annually. Usually, the DOT inspection sticker or label is placed somewhere near the front of the trailer. You must review this label or sticker for EVERY trailer you hook to, to ensure it has been inspected within the last 11 months. NEVER pull a trailer that has not been inspected within the last 11 months.

SECTION FIVE
Hours of Service
The Driving Clock

The duty you perform will not only consist of driving. There are various other activities you will perform throughout the day and the week. You will be required to log your activities on the ELD. You are also required to carry a paper logbook in the tractor in the event the ELD malfunction, yet you still need to drive and/or perform On-Duty activities. Never record status changes on the ELD and in a paper logbook simultaneously. Only use a paper logbook when the ELD is unusable, and approved by the log department and your Driver Manager or Dispatcher.

LOGGING IN AND OUT OF THE ELD

You will have to log in on the ELD, with ever truck you drive, before you drive. Each ELD will have a log in screen where you can type certain information in, so that you are able to log driving time and on-duty time under your name.

Note: Never drive a truck while logged out! You must log in first, and log a pre-trip inspection before you are legally able to drive. You are still required to visually and physically pre-trip the truck and trailer along with electronically logging it on the ELD.

HOW TO USE THE ELD

The usage of the ELD is how the company will know what you are doing without having to constantly call or send messages on the ELD. These activities, including driving, will be timed through a system called the Hours of Service. The Hours of Service is a way to organize on-duty and off-duty time, and to allow drivers time to work and time to rest from on-duty activities. Below is a breakdown of how the Hours of Service is systemized.

Note: The 60-hour and 70-hour drive week will not be described in this guidebook. Refer to your employer with regard to driving under a 70-hour or 60-hour work week.

70-HOUR CLOCK (TOTAL ON-DUTY/DRIVE TIME)
– After being home and starting your week, you will have a full 70-hour clock to start with. As you drive and perform work related duties under the 'On-Duty' and 'Driving' statuses, time will be drawn from the 70-hour clock. When the 70-hour clock is close to 00:00, you will need to perform a 34-hour reset to receive a full 70-hour clock again. A 34-hour reset is being under the 'sleeper berth' or 'off-duty' status for at least 34 consecutive hours.

14-HOUR DRAW (DAILY ON-DUTY TIME) – Each workday, you will begin with 14-hours of 'On-Duty' work time as long as you were under the Sleeper Berth status for at least 10 consecutive hours. As you perform duties while under the 'On-Duty' status, time will be drawn from the 14-hour on-duty time and 70-hour clock. Always park in a safe, legal area and enter the 'Sleeper Berth' status before the 14-hour clock reaches 00:00.

11-HOUR DRAW (TOTAL DAILY DRIVE TIME) –
You are allowed to drive a maximum of 11 hours per day out of the available 14-hour on-duty time. As you drive, time will be drawn from the total 70-hour clock, daily 14-hour on-duty time, and the 11-hour daily drive time. Always park in a safe, legal area and enter the 'Sleeper Berth' status before the 11-hour drive time reaches 00:00.

8-HOUR DRAW (STARTING DAILY DRIVE TIME) –
You will begin each day with 8 out of the 11-hour drive time. You will need to take a minimum 30-minute break in 'Off-Duty' or 'Sleeper Berth' to gain the rest of the 11-hour drive time and 14-hour on-duty time.

30-MINUTE BREAK – A minimum of 30 minutes under 'Off-Duty' or 'Sleeper Berth' will add the rest of the available hours from the 14-hour on-duty time, and 11-hour drive time.

Try to arrive at the shipper and consignee with a full clock or at least enough time to perform all the duties you will need to while at the shipper and consignee including getting loaded or unloaded. It could take 20 minutes or a few hours to get loaded or unloaded at a shipper or receiver depending on circumstances and timing.

Always leave yourself a time cushion. Never run the clock low. Conserve your drive time and on-duty time by switching to 'On-Duty' and 'Off-Duty' when appropriate. It is wise to begin looking for a place to park at the end of the day when you have 1 and a half to 2 hours left on the clock. Make sure you switch to 'Sleeper Birth' right after you park at the end of the day so that the clock does not run out and put you in HOS violation. It is easy to park and then get distracted (or simply forget) and not switch to 'Sleeper Birth' at the end of your day.

SWITCHING DUTIES

There are four options on the ELD Hours of Service screen that you can select from. They are each a 'status'. They serve an important purpose, and they should be well understood. Below is a breakdown of the purpose of each status option.

SLEEPER BERTH – Select this status at the end of your driving before the clock reaches 00:00. When you are not driving, not performing any work-related duties, and you are near the end of your 14-hour clock, select this status. 10 consecutive hours under "Sleeper Berth" will reset the 11-hour drive time and the 14-hour on-duty time. If you physically will not be in the sleeper berth while on a 10-hour reset, you must log 'Off-Duty'.

ON DUTY – Select this status when performing work related duties which are NOT driving. There is a place to add remarks when you switch to 'On-Duty'. Add a remark if necessary, and then click 'OK' or 'CONTINUE'.

DRIVING – The ELD may mark you under this status automatically anytime the truck is moving (except below 5 MPH). Some trucks might not switch over automatically, and you will need to manually switch to the 'Driving' status before physically driving the truck. If you need to move the truck below 5 MPH, always manually switch the ELD to 'Driving'. After you have moved the truck to where you want it to be, then you can switch it back to one of the other three statuses.

OFF DUTY – Select this status anytime you stop to take a break, get food, use the restroom, or any non-driving and non-work-related activities. When you take home time, log 'Off-Duty' if you will not be in the sleeper berth.

REMARKS ON THE ELD

When switching statuses, there will be an option to add remarks to the status change. 'On-Duty' + 'Pre-Trip Inspection' is a common one. Adding remarks to your status changes allow the company you work for to know what you are physically doing without them being there in person. Below is a breakdown of the purpose of each remark. The company you work for may have different or special remarks which are not listed here.

NOTE: It is illegal to idle the truck around attempting to avoid the ELD from switching the status to 'Driving'. You must manually switch the status to 'Driving' if you need to move the truck for whatever reason.

PRE-TRIP INSPECTION – You must log at least 15 minutes 'On-Duty' + 'Pre-Trip Inspection' on the ELD each day before you drive. You still need to inspect the tractor and trailer visually and physically in addition to electronically logging it on the ELD.

POST-TRIP INSPECTION – Similar to Pre-Trip Inspection, log this remark at the end of your driving day while you are inspecting the tractor and trailer before leaving to go home or entering the sleeper berth for the night.

FUEL – Select this remark whenever you are adding natural gas, diesel fuel, reefer fuel, and/or DEF to the tanks.

LOAD AND UNLOAD – Select when you are at a stop-off/pickup, or when you will get loaded and unloaded simultaneously. This occurs whenever the gross weight is over 80,000 pounds and the shipper must take some weight off by removing and adding items with different weight. It also happens when the weight distribution is putting one or more axles over the legal limit. The shipper will need to move the items around inside the trailer to shift the weight distribution.

LOAD – When you are at any shipper getting live-loaded, you must select this remark. Note: some companies may not have a 'hook' option in the remarks section. You will have to use this remark as a substitute when hooking to trailers.

UNLOAD – Select when you are at the consignee getting live-unloaded. Note: some companies may not have a 'drop' option in the remarks section. You will have to use this remark as a substitute when dropping trailers.

DROP – Any time you drop a trailer, whether loaded or empty, add this remark to your On-Duty status.

HOOK – Select this remark when you hook to a trailer, whether it is empty or loaded.

DOT INSPECTION – If you ever get pulled over or stopped by DOT or law enforcement for an inspection or any other reason, you MUST select this remark along with the 'On-Duty' status.

HOME TIME – Log this remark along with the 'Sleeper Birth' or 'Off-Duty' status whenever you are taking time home and away from your driving/work duties.

MAINTENANCE – If the tractor or trailer is in the shop or getting serviced, add this remark along with 'On-Duty' or 'Off-Duty' status. Contact your Driver Manager or Dispatch with regard on what to log for truck maintenance.

SEEKING SAFE HAVEN – Select this remark if the weather is unsatisfactory (snowing, heavy winds, ext.) to drive or you have been in a collision or incident.

BREAK DOWN – If the tractor and/or trailer you are driving has problems, park in a safe area and select 'On-Duty' along with this remark.

30-MINUTE BREAK – To receive the rest of your available drive time, you will need to log at least 30 minutes 'Off-Duty' or 'Sleeper Berth' along with this remark. If the ELD you are using does not have this option, then switch to 'Off-Duty' or 'Sleeper Berth' for at least 30 minutes.

CHARGING – There will come a time when all-electric commercial motor vehicles (known as CEVs) will be common on the highway and need to be charged. Select this remark along with 'On-Duty', 'Off-Duty', or 'Sleeper Berth' whenever the truck is hooked to a charging device.

RECAP HOURS

Each day you log 'Driving' and 'On-Duty' on the ELD, the hours are bulked and saved in the system. Whatever hours were logged 8 days ago, you will receive those same hours as On-Duty time and drive time. If you drove 7 hours and logged 2 hours 'On-Duty' 8 days ago, on the current day you will receive a total of 9 hours. Out of those 9 hours, you can perform driving and On-Duty activities. It is possible to drive and perform On-Duty activities for weeks using recap hours.

PAY PER DIEM (PAY LESS TAXES)

Most people are not aware just how much money never see their bank account due to taxes. Even though they have worked a full-time job, gotten a raise, or worked over-time, their check still does not look as big as it should. With jobs, the more money you earn, the higher the tax bracket, and the more money you pay in taxes. This can be maddening, you want all (or at least most) of the wages you have earned.

 Fortunately in trucking there is a way around this. It is called Pay Per Diem. Most trucking companies will have a pay program you can sign up for after you begin driving with them. Usually you will have to call someone from the company or go on the company website to sign up. But what is Pay Per Diem?

 Basically it places you in a lower tax bracket by restricting a certain amount or percentage of your income to 'non-taxable'. This means that a certain amount of your income cannot be taxed. This will make a smaller portion of your income free to be taxed, meaning that LESS taxes will be taken out of your check. For example, lets say a driver earns $2,000 a week as a tanker driver. That entire $2,000 will be subjected to taxes. But he (or she) decided to sign up for Pay Per Diem at the company they drive for.

 The company's rate is 13%, meaning 13% of the $2,000 cannot be taxed. That is $260 a week that cannot be taxed and go straight to their bank account! That would mean only $1,740 can be taxed. This does not sound like much, but over the months and years it add up to A LOT of money saved. You likely will also get more money back (or owe much less) when you do your taxes.

Please sign up for your company's Pay Per Diem and earn more money than other drivers who do not know about this! Keep those checks higher and more money in your bank account! Speaking of more money, here is another one:

NOT BY THE MILE, BUT BY TIME

I learned something very important withing the first few months of driving as a solo driver before I became a mentor. I realized that companies who pay by the mile, really do pay by the mile. But the thing is, since you are getting paid by the mile, you are ONLY getting paid when ever you are actually driving (with an empty or loaded trailer). Many truck companies don't pay for On Duty time (unfortunately, whether it is or is not legal for them to do so).

If you take excessively long lunch breaks, take a long time to hook or drop trailers, or wander around at the truck stops, you may find that your paychecks are not very high. The longer the truck sits without you driving, the less money you are getting paid, literally. Of course this does not mean to go over the speed limit, skip pre-trips, or run stop signs. Definitely don't do those things! You still have to follow all road rules and regulations and DOT laws. Never break the law in a CMV or any other vehicle.

But what this means is that you need to be safe, legal, efficient, and fast when you are doing your job. While mentoring, I would time the students for things such as fueling, hooking to trailers, dropping trailers, time looking for parking, lunch breaks, and other similar things that are 'On Duty' or lunch break activities but not actually driving. I realized that the students commonly took 4 to 8 times as long to perform similar activities in comparison to me, literally.

If it only took me 2 minutes to unhook and drop a trailer, it took them 8 to 15 minutes! Usually it's because they struggles to unhook the connections, drop the landing gear, or they would somehow end up on the phone and lost track of time. As mentor I had to keep on the look out for these, as not only do drivers lose money from taking excessively long time for these types of activities, but so do truck companies.

You want to be safe, legal, and to the job right. But at some point, it become pure laziness, carelessness, or just plain taking too long. If the company you drive for pay you by the mile, you will have to come up with a system of performing your job so that you are not wasting time unnecessarily. Keep the truck moving, and you'll keep your paychecks high!

DETENTION PAY (YOU ARE ENTITLED)

If you are an owner-operator or truck fleet owner, you likely know what detention pay is and how to obtain it. If you are a company driver, it is likely that the company you work for will never tell you anything about detention pay. They may prefer to pocket the funds or decide not to pay you detention pay if they do not receive detention pay from the shipper/receiver.

But you are legally entitled to receive detention pay if the shipper or receiver take longer than 2 hours to live load or live unload your trailer. Shippers and receivers are obligated to load and unload trailers within 2 hours, meaning the driver is waiting for the shipper or receiver to finish loading/unloading before the driver can leave.

The company you drive for may have an automatic system that will add the detention pay to your check or direct deposit it to your checking account on file. Other companies may have a form you must fill out to receive the detention pay. But there are companies which will never mention it to you, and it will be up to you to record the necessary information and send it to your Driver Manager (or Dispatcher) as well as the Payroll Department.

Ensure that you are logged 'On-Duty' and using the appropriate remark whenever you are getting live loaded or unloaded; request detention pay after the loading/unloading is complete.

Below is a general template you can write to request detention pay if the company you work for does not have an automatic payout system or detention pay form.

REQUESTING DETENTION PAY
DRIVER CODE:
LOAD#:
TRUCK#:
TRAILER#:
SHIPPER NAME:
LOCATOIN:
DATE:
START TIME:
END TIME:
TOTAL TIME:
STATUS:
ACTIVITY:

DRIVER PAY - HOURLY, BY THE MILE, OR BY THE LOAD

Depending on the duties you perform, the loads you are dispatched on, the type of driving you perform, and the company you drive for, there are various ways to receive the funds for the duties you perform.

If you will be paid hourly, it won't matter how many miles you drive or what loads you pull. Your pay will be by the hour. If you wish to earn more, you will need to drive more hours and perform on-duty activities for a longer period of time. If you will be paid by-the-mile, you will be paid for the miles you drive, and not by the number of hours. The more miles you drive, the more money you will earn. But know what miles you get paid and which you do not. Some companies may not pay for miles while you are bobtailing or driving an empty trailer.

If you are going to be paid by the load, the amount you receive will be fixed and based on the load itself, and not the hours or miles driven. If getting paid by the load, and you are an owner operator, it is important to know if the load payout will cover expenses (such as fuel, tolls, truck

Hours of Service: The Driving Clock | **41**

insurance, truck payment, ext.) while leaving some left over as profit.

ZIP CODE TO ZIP CODE PAY

Many drivers have complained about this type of pay structure. The reason is that zip codes vary in size and length along your route. It is common for drivers to be paid very low wages while driving zip code to zip code. You could lose from 10% to as much as 50% of your earnings.

    This type of pay structure also has a profound effect on your taxable income and could make it difficult to meet certain financial qualifications. Hub miles (actual miles driven while loaded), also known as loaded miles, is more accurate and offer a less complicated pay structure. If you are working for a company that pay zip code to zip code, ensure that you are aware of their compensation structure and policies. Ensure that you are getting paid for the work you do and miles you drive and not 'shortchanged'.

    Zip code to zip code pay is not illegal (at the time this book was published) or necessarily wrong, but it can be different than you expect.

SECTION SIX
ELD Macros

ELD stands for 'Electronic Logging Device'. The ELD is the little brother (newer) of the paper logbook. ELDs came about to help simplify logging hours of service, communication between driver and company staff, and prevention fraudulent logging of hours and drive time. All commercial motor vehicles are required to have a functioning ELD installed in the tractor (certain exemptions apply, which are not explained or listed in this guidebook).

Macros are organized, pre-structured messages that you fill in with information and send into the computer system. This is how others can keep track of where you are and what you are doing.

Your driving duties will not only consist of driving, but you will also have to send macros using the ELD. They are easy to fill in. There are a variety of macros, and each is numbered and named. Fill and send macros only while you are parked in a safe location and in a time appropriate manner.

If the ELD ever shut off or malfunction, contact your Driver Manager or the log department. Usually, the ELD will shut off after the tractor has been parked for a while with the engine off. Ask your Driver Manager what procedure they want you to follow for turning on the ELD.

Here are the basic macros you will find on the ELD that you will use most often. There are other macros which are not listed here. Review the manual which comes with the tractor's permit book to understand how to use the other macros. Contact you driver manager about them as well if you need help.

00 – FREEFORM
Type a random message from scratch using the keyboard on the ELD's screen.

01 – LOAD CONFIRMATION
Send only once when you receive a new load or empty pickup load assignment in the inbox. The load assignment has all the information of the load you are dispatched on such as the load number, shipper name, shipper address, consignee address, and the time the load need to be delivered. Ensure that you are not sending a load confirmation for a 'load preview'. Load previews will have 00 and 000 where it says 'empty miles' and 'loaded miles' on the load page. This is perhaps Lorena's favorite macro! It's because she gets to drive on the interstate, her favorite thing to do! Ha!

02 – ARRIVED AT SHIPPER
Send when you arrive to pick up an empty trailer, pre-loaded trailer, or to get live-loaded.

03 – LOADED AT SHIPPER
Send after you have hooked to an empty trailer, pre-loaded trailer, or you are finished getting live-loaded at the shipper.

04 – ARRIVED AT PICK-UP/STOPOFF
A pick-up/stop-off is a location you drive to before you drive to the consignee. At the pick-up/stop-off location, the shipper will either add or take some of the load out of the trailer, or a combination of both. If you get a load that has a pick-up/stop-off, send this macro when you arrive at the location. If the load you have been dispatched on has a pick-up/stop-off, you will see '01' or '02' next to 'pick-ups/stop-offs' on the load page you have received in the inbox.

05 – DEPARTED PICK-UP/STOPOFF
Send this macro when you are finished getting loaded/unloaded at the pick-up/stop-off location.

06 – ARRIVED AT CONSIGNEE
The consignee is the drop off (or unloading) location. Send this macro when you arrive at the consignee. You will either drop the loaded trailer in a designated parking space, dock drop the trailer (dock the trailer at a door and then unhook from it), or get live-unloaded at the consignee.

07 – EMPTY AT CONSIGNEE
Send this when you have dropped a loaded trailer or finished getting live-unloaded at the consignee.

08 – T-CALL
A T-Call is when you don't take a loaded trailer or empty trailer all the way to the consignee, but instead you drop it at a location that is not the same location as the consignee. Send this macro after you drop the trailer. Make sure you place a copy of the BOL and any other important paperwork inside the nosebox of the trailer. If there is no nosebox, or the cover is missing, you may have to take a bag or container, place the BOL inside the bag or container, and tie it the landing gear near the crank handle. Ensure it is place where it will not get wet if it rains or snows. Note the location you have placed the paperwork in the comments section of this macro, so the next driver know where to find the paperwork.

09 – TRAILER CHANGE
Changing trailers is easy, often called a 'trailer swap' or 'repower'. This is when your Dispatcher or Driver Manager want you to meet another driver at a specific location to swap trailers and BOLs. You will drop your trailer and give your BOL to the other driver. The other driver will drop his/her trailer and give you their BOLs. You will hook to their trailer, and they will hook to yours. You are

essentially swapping trailers and BOLs. Send this after you are hooked to the new trailer and have the new BOL.

11 – TIME OFF REQUEST

Send this at least a few days before you want to go home. Speak with your Driver Manager or Dispatcher to negotiate home time.

13 – UPDATE PTA

Send this macro if you think you will arrive at the consignee at a different time due to traffic, bad weather, emergency tractor or trailer issues, ext.

NOTE: Utilize the comments section at the bottom of each macro to freehand notes if necessary.

LEGAL DISCLAIMER: "Never type cuss words, slang, derogatory remarks, profanity, or unprofessional statements in the comments section. The author and Johnson Craftworks LLC relinquish liability."

Also, there may come a time when an 'Arrived At Charging Station' and a 'Departed From Charging Station' will be added to the ELD for the usage of all-electric tractors (CEVs) and electric trailers and their need to keep the batteries charged.

SECTION SEVEN
The 5TH Wheel

No, the 5th wheel isn't actually a wheel. But it sure is one of the most important parts of a tractor-trailer! It is actually a mechanism with a round shape that pivots on the horizontal axis (and somewhat from side to side). It also allow hooking and unhooking of trailers to the tractor unit.

Pivoting of the tractor and trailer combination is possible by hooking the trailer to the tractor at a fixed point (center of the 5th wheel), while grease between the 5th wheel plate and bottom of the trailer allow rotation on the horizontal axis.

FIXED VS ADJUSTABLE 5TH WHEEL

Most 5th wheels are adjustable, but there are tractors with fixed 5th wheels. If it is fixed, you will be unable to adjust the location of the 5th wheel on the tractor. Adjustable versions allow the location of its placement to vary. If the tractor you operate has an adjustable unit, it is important to know how to adjust its placement.

LEGAL DISCLAIMER: "Always follow your company's policy with regard to sliding the 5th wheel, and always make the adjustment according to how it is described in the tractor's factory manual. The author and Johnson Craftworks LLC relinquish liability."

Below is a basic and general method of sliding the 5th wheel on modern tractors. You will need to hook to an empty trailer and lower the landing gear all the way to the ground.

SLIDING THE 5TH WHEEL

1. While hooked to an empty trailer, make sure the air and electrical lines are disconnected and properly

secured to a location on the tractor. Make sure the landing gear is all the way DOWN. The feet (aka shoes) of the landing gear need to touch the ground.

2. Drop the tractor's air bags. Ensure the tractor is in neutral and the YELLOW KNOB is pulled out. Next, get out of the tractor and check to see if there is space between the 5th wheel and the trailer. If you can see daylight, lower the trailer only enough to close the gap, so that you do not see any daylight.

3. Engage the 5th wheel slide button, switch, or lever, which should be somewhere inside the cab.

4. Push in the YELLOW BUTTON to release the parking brake.

5. If you need the 5th wheel slid to the back, drive forward. If you need the 5th wheel slid to the front, drive in reverse.

6. If the tractor does not move, the pins might be 'stuck'. Rock the tractor back and forth by driving forward and then backward until the pins release and the tractor move.

7. When you have slid the 5th wheel in the desired position, pull out the YELLOW KNOB and shift the tractor into neutral.

8. Get out and look at the 5th wheel to ensure it is in the position you want it to be.

9. Repeat steps 4 through 8 until the 5th wheel is in the desired position.

10. Once you get the 5th wheel in the desired position, engage the 5th wheel slide button to lock the pins. If the pins do not lock, you may need to drive forward or backward so that the pins can realign and lock.

11. Raise the air bags. Follow the process of unhooking from a trailer and drop the trailer if you do not need to take it. Make sure that you lower the landing gear again all the way DOWN until the feet touch the ground, then drop the trailer.

LOCATION OF THE 5TH WHEEL IS IMPORTANT

The location of the 5th wheel affect the drivability of the tractor when a trailer is hooked. It changes the turning radius and driving space. Too far up (toward the tractor's engine) and the side of the tractor could damage the side of the trailer while making a turn or performing an alley dock. Too far back (away from the engine) and turns may be more difficult or require more space. The airlines and electrical connections could be pulled if they are too short or hung improperly.

Further up make turns easier and reduce air drag, which slightly improves fuel efficiency. Further back increase 'tractor jerk'. Tractor jerk can cause a tractor-trailer to lose control on icy, wet, or dusty roads by 'pushing' the tractor and causing the drive wheels to lose traction while making turns or going over a hill.

This is because too much weight is located toward the rear of the tractor, and this create more leverage on the drive axles. The higher leverage cause energy to focus in the area of the drive axles and could cause a loss of control on icy roads. Ensure that you are not turning at too high a speed to prevent tractor jerk from happening.

The location also affect the weight distribution amongst the axles of the tractor. If the 5th wheel is closer to the front (toward the engine), more weight will be placed on the steer wheels. Further toward the back (away from the engine) and more weight will be placed on the drive axles. Ensure when sliding the 5th wheel that it does not cause the tractor-trailer to be overweight on any axle while a loaded trailer is hooked.

GREASING THE 5TH WHEEL

Ever got stuck under a trailer with the wheels spinning while trying to unhook? It is common for tractor-trailer drivers to not regrease the 5th wheel plate. A dry 5th wheel plate make it difficult to hook and unhook from trailers. The metal-to-metal contact of the plate and bottom of the trailer can cause high friction, which can cause grabbing of the 5th wheel and trailer.

The plate could also be damaged by the high friction. Grease on the plate lower friction, and make it easy to slide under and out from trailers. 5th wheel grease can be purchased from truck stops. Contact the company you drive for and ask if the purchase of 5th wheel grease for the tractor will be reimbursed.

It may help to spread the grease around on the 5th wheel plate for a wider coverage area and less runoff (or 'pushoff' from the front of the trailer pushing the grease off the plate).

REGREASING 5TH WHEEL

Depending on the design of the 5th wheel, grease will get pushed to the sides of the plate. Instead of constantly buying new grease, it is possible to use a putty knife or spoon to scrape off grease from the sides and place back on the plate of the 5th wheel. This will save time and money. Ensure there is no dirt or debris in the grease you are recycling.

SECTION EIGHT
Hook & Drop Trailers

Unlike box trucks where the box is attached directly to the cab, with tractors, you must attach to a trailer. The trailer is separate from the tractor. The tractor is the powered engine and cab unit. If you wish to take a load, you are required to be hooked to an empty trailer and get live loaded, or you will need to hook to a pre-loaded trailer. In this chapter you will learn about hooking and dropping trailers, both empty and loaded.

BASICS OF HOOKING TO TRAILERS

You must perform a pre-trip inspection on every trailer you hook to, whether it is empty or pre-loaded. Make sure that you log on the ELD 'On-Duty' + 'Pre-Trip Inspection' (or 'Load') when hooking to trailers and containers. Containers will be discussed later in this chapter.

Never hook directly to a trailer without checking the space between the 5th wheel and trailer. It may be necessary to get out and look a few times to ensure that the 5th wheel is completely under the trailer, but not hooked to it. It is possible for a trailer to be dropped very high to where you could get stuck under the trailer if the 5th wheel is not flat with no space when hooking. In this situation, the 5th wheel could completely miss the king pin, and you could damage the back of the tractor or trailer by backing too far.

Not all tractors are the same physical height. Your tractor may be lower or higher than other tractors, and this will affect the high of the trailer when dropped. You want the front of the 5th wheel to be aligned with the front of the trailer. You will need to use the driver side mirror to look at the trailer and rear of the tractor to determine the correct location.

If the 5th wheel is not flat, you will need to lower the trailer using the landing gear handle until there is no space between the 5th wheel and trailer. Once there is no space, and you have performed a pre-trip inspection on the trailer, you can hook to the trailer if the trailer passes the pre-trip inspection. Always back gently to hook to the trailer. There is no need to ram into the trailer or back aggressively while hooking. All that is needed is for the locking jaw in the 5th wheel to latch around the trailer's kingpin and lock.

After you have hooked to the trailer, perform a tug test. ALWAYS PERFORM A TUG TEST! The last thing you want is to perform a pre-trip on the trailer, hook, and drive off only for the trailer to smash onto the frame of the truck! You don't want to drop the trailer and it hit the wheels and cause damage to the drivetrain of the tractor, or drop the trailer on the ground.

HOOKING TO EMPTY AND PRELOADED TRAILERS

Before hooking to an empty trailer, always check the inside of the trailer to ensure it is actually empty. Never assume it is empty, it may actually be loaded! Also check to see if there is any trash or debris inside the trailer that you may need to clean out before you arrive to the next location.

After you have finished, you can hook all of the connections and raise the landing gear. Always raise landing gear all the way up when hooking to trailers. Always get the BOL (paperwork) before you leave the shipper, and check that the seal is attached, locked, and the seal number match what is on the BOL. Some shippers will provide you the BOL and seal after you have hooked to the trailer and drive to the checkout location.

HOOKING AT AN ANGLE

Dirty jokes aside, you may find yourself in a situation where the trailer you want to get is in a difficult location to hook in a straight line. You will need to hook to the trailer at an angle. To do this, the middle of the 5th wheel will need to be aimed toward the king pin. You will need to get out and look a few times to ensure that the middle of the 5th wheel is aimed toward the kingpin.

Do not ram the trailer or back aggressively when hooking to a trailer at an angle. You will need to get the 5th wheel under the trailer without hooking to check for spacing between the 5th wheel and trailer. If there is no space, then you can hook to the trailer. Note that the trailer may move a few inches (or feet) from its original location. Ensure that the trailer will not hit another truck, trailer, building, person, or anything else that may cause damage or a fatality.

Below is a basic and general step-by-step process for hooking to a trailer. **LEGAL DISCLAIMER:** "Always follow your company's policy with regard to hooking to trailers. Always follow your Driver Manager's recommendations. The author and Johnson Craftworks LLC relinquish liability."

PROCEDURE FOR HOOKING TO TRAILERS

1. Align the tractor with the trailer while backing.

2. Get the 5th wheel under the trailer, DO NOT HOOK right away!

3. Get out and check the spacing between the 5th wheel and trailer. Lower the trailer if there is space, until no daylight can be seen between the 5th wheel and trailer.

4. Perform a complete pre-trip inspection of the trailer. If nothing is damage, missing, broken, or out of date, go to the next step. If you find something wrong, contact your Driver Manager.

5. Hook to the trailer and perform a tug test. If you skip this step, when you drive forward, the trailer will drop and hit the frame of the tractor or hit the ground. DO NOT SKIP THIS STEP. ALWAYS DO A TUG TEST WHEN HOOKING TO A TRAILER to ensure the 5th wheel's locking jaw is latched and locked around the king pin.

6. Hook the airlines and electrical cable. (If you are operating an all-electric tractor, there may be a 4th line to connect for the battery/solar charging unit on electric trailers).

7. Walk around the tractor and trailer counter-clockwise to check all the lights that they work. If all lights work, go to the next step. If a light is out, damaged, or missing, notify your Driver Manager.

8. Get in the tractor and push in the RED KNOB only (to air up the trailer tandems). If you skip this step, you may find yourself struggling to slide the tandems, and you will not be able to check for air leaks. Give the tandems 2 to 3 minutes to air up after pushing in the RED KNOB.

9. While the trailer tandems are airing up, bring up the landing gear, and secure the handle on the handle mount.

10. If the tandems do not have a leak, get in the tractor, and pull out the RED KNOB so you can slide the tandems.

11. Go to the rear of the trailer, where the tandems are, and release the tandem locking pins (by pushing/pulling the button, or pulling out the handle). The tractor you are driving may also have a switch or button inside the cab to actuate the tandem locking pins.

12. Get back into the truck. Put the tractor into reverse, and push in the YELLOW KNOB only. Then back the trailer until you feel and hear a bump sound, indicating that the tandems have slid all the way forward. Never ram the tandems or back aggressively. A gentle bump is all that is needed. (ensure there is nothing behind the trailer that you might hit while sliding the tandems to the front.)

13. Shift into neutral and out the YELLOW KNOB.

14. Go to the back of the trailer, where the tandems are, and lock the tandem locking pins (by pulling/pushing the button, or releasing/pushing in the handle). The tractor you are driving may also have a button or switch on the inside of the cab to actuate the tandem locking pins.

15. If the locking pins do not push out to lock, you will need to get into the tractor, shift into drive, push in the YELLOW KNOB. Drive forward, then backward one time to align the pins so they will lock. Once the pins lock, pull out the YELLOW KNOB. If you are ready to drive off, then you can push in both knobs.

16. Push in the RED KNOB. The RED KNOB is not a parking brake, and should always be pressed in when a trailer is hooked. The only time the RED KNOB can be out is when you are sliding the tandems, getting live loaded or unloaded, or ready to drop a trailer. If you are ready to drive off, then you can push in both knobs.

CONTAINERS VS DRY VANS

There may come a time that you get dispatched on a load that require you to hook to a container. Containers are different than dry vans in a few ways. Usually, containers have the landing gear crank handle on the passenger side.

The position of the kingpin will look different than that of a dry van due to the container drop frame extending further than the container.

You will be required to slide the 5th wheel ALL THE WAY TO THE BACK (away from the tractor's engine) to hook to a container. Not doing so could cause the tractor to hit the side of the container and cause damage while making turns or performing an alley dock.

Containers also have a different location for the glad hands located on the drop frame. The location is much lower than that of a dry van. Because of this, they are prone to tearing the lines and cables from the tractor or dop frame while making a tight turn. Depending on the design of your tractor and the hangar mechanism, you may not have to slide the 5th wheel all the way to the back on day cab tractors and short sleeper cab tractors.

ADJUSTING THE HANGARS TO SUIT CONTAINERS

It is necessary to readjust the hangars for the airlines and electrical cable after hooking to a container. You need to ensure that the airlines and electrical cable do not hang too low, so that they do not catch on anything while making turns. You will also need to add an additional hangar to the airlines and electrical cable. Then you can adjust both hangars so that the lines and cable can stretch longer, but without hanging too low.

Extra hangars can be purchased at a truck stop. You may need to purchase two packages of the hangar and link them together, so that the original hangar on the truck is short, and the linked hangar is longer, depending on the tractor you are driving. It helps to also have the extra clips from the additional hangar to fine tune the length of each hangar.

DROPPING TRAILERS

Once you are able to safely hook to trailers, you should know how to also drop trailers. Park trailers parallel with the parking space and not crooked. Park and drop the trailer so that the front of the trailer is lined up with the front of the trailers next to it unless there is not enough space behind the trailer to back far enough.

LEGAL DISCLAIMER: "Always follow your company's policies and Driver Manager's recommendations with regard to dropping trailers. Always follow the security clerk, shipping clerk, and shipper's directions on where and how to drop trailers. The author and Johnson Craftworks LLC relinquish liability."

NOTE: When dropping loaded trailers of 30,000 lbs. or more, it is recommended you detach from the trailer and pull forward just a little so that the 5th wheel is still under the trailer. Then lower the tractor's air bags for at least 20 seconds before driving completely out from under the trailer. Loaded trailers over 30,000 lbs. could drop lower than empty trailers (especially on dirt or gravel lots) and cause the trailer to slam onto the frame or wheels of the tractor.

NOTE: Make sure each time you park to drop a trailer that you switch to 'On-Duty' + 'Drop' (or 'Unload') on the ELD.

PROCEDURE FOR DROPPING TRAILERS

1. Back or pull the trailer into the desired parking space, ensuring you do not hit anything. Park the trailer so that the front of the trailer is lined up with the front of the trailers next to it.

2. Pull out BOTH KNOBS, and shift the tractor into neutral.

3. Get out and ensure that you have not hit anything, then disconnect the airlines and the electrical cable from the trailer, and secure them to the tractor.

4. Bring the landing gear ALL THE WAY DOWN until the landing gear feet (aka shoes) are firm on the ground. Do not overturn the handle to where it is difficult to turn. The landing gear feet only need to be directly touching the ground with no space.

5. If the tractor does not have an electronic 5th wheel release, then pull the 5th wheel release handle to unlock the 5th wheel's locking jaw from the kingpin of the trailer. If the handle will not come out, you will need to get into the tractor, and reverse to release the pressure off the 5th wheel's locking jaw so that the 5th wheel can unlock. Park and shift the transmission into neutral after you have reversed to take pressure off the 5th wheel's locking jaw.

6. Engage the 5th wheel release button, switch, or lever.

7. Shift the transmission into drive (or forward gear for manual transmissions) and only push in the YELLOW KNOB. Drive forward and drop the trailer.

It is important that the landing gear feet are touching the ground and there is no space between the bottom of the feet and the ground. When you pull from under the trailer and drop it, the trailer will actually drop lower than where it was while it was hooked to the tractor. If you don't drop the landing gear all the way to the ground, when you pull from under the trailer, it could smash the frame of the tractor or the wheels.

USING AN ELECTRONIC 5TH WHEEL RELEASE

There are four tried and true steps that work 100% of the time when dropping a trailer with an electronic 5th wheel release. Look in the tractor's manual to see how to safely operate the tractor's electronic 5th wheel release. If you perform these four steps and the 5th wheel won't release, the 5th wheel itself or its components may need service. Contact your Driver Manager if you have issues releasing the 5th wheel, or if the 5th wheel is damaged, or has damaged/malfunctioning components.

PROCEDURE FOR USING ELECTRONIC 5TH WHEEL RELEASE

1. **REVERSE** – Before actuating the button, reverse and back just a little to take pressure off the 5th wheel's locking jaw before engaging the 5th wheel release button. Not reversing before engaging the 5th wheel release button may keep the 5th wheel's locking jaw from unlocking.

2. **PARK** – After reversing, immediately pull out the YELLOW BUTTON and shift the tractor into neutral.

3. **BUTTON** – Engage the 5th wheel release button.

4. **DRIVE FORWARD** – When the 5th wheel's locking jaw has been unlocked, drive forward to drop the trailer.

DROPPING AT AN ANGLE

It is recommended you never drop a trailer at an angle. The trailer's tail end could move several inches to a few feet and hit an object, another tractor, trailer, or person. If you need to drop a trailer at an angle for whatever reason, it is recommended you ensure that the tail end of the trailer has enough space to move, in case when pulling from under the trailer, it does move. The landing gear must be all the way to the ground, and touching the ground when dropping at an angle.

SECTION NINE
Sliding Tandems

I remember the first time I had to slide the tandems on a trailer. I just couldn't get them to move. I tried everything. Except one thing. I never aired up the tandems after I hooked to the trailer. The red knob was out the whole time. I sat in the seat looking at the red knob and realized that the trailer need to be aired up for the tandems to receive air for the air bag suspension, self-inflation system (for the tires), and of course sliding the tandems. The tandems have pins, gears, levers, and/or locks which need air to move.

I pushed in the red knob and waited 3 minutes. The air gauge on the digital cluster dropped a little before the air compressor turned on to rebuild the air pressure. I then pulled out the red knob, actuated the tandem release handle, and the tandems slide quickly and smoothy as if they were riding on a rail of grease! Ha!

NOTES ON SLIDING TANDEMS

Always supply air to the trailer (to air up the tandems) before attempting to slide the tandems. If the tandems won't slide, they may be rusted stiff. You'll need to rock the trailer forward and backward by switching from drive to reverse a few times.

Sliding the tandems to the front make tight turns easier without hitting anything, but loading and unloading of the trailer is rough for forklift operators. Sliding the tandems to the rear make tight turns more difficult with a higher risk of hitting curbs and objects on the inside of the turn, but make loading and unloading of the trailer smooth for forklift operators.

Just a gentle bump is all that is needed when sliding tandems. The tandem locking pins are actuated by a button, lever, or switch near the tandems (some tractors have a button inside the cab).

Sliding the tandems will adjust the weight distribution on all axles. If the tandems are all the way in the back, the weight will shift onto the steer and drive axles of the tractor. If the tandems are all the way in the front, the weight will shift onto the tandems. Ensure when sliding the tandems that you are within legal axle weight limits. Maximum axle weights and using weigh scales will be discussed in the next chapter of this guidebook.

LEGAL DISCLAIMER: "Always slide tandems according to your company's policy, Driver Manager's recommendations, the shipping clerk, security officer, shipper, and receiver's directions. The author and Johnson Craftworks LLC relinquish liability."

PROCEDURE FOR SLIDING TANDEMS FORWARD

You will need to slide the tandems forward after hooking to a trailer. This help in making turns without the trailer wheels hitting curbs.

1. When you are in a safe area to slide the tandems, pull out BOTH KNOBS and make sure the tractor is in neutral.

2. Get out of the tractor, and go to the back of the trailer to ensure nothing is behind the trailer that you would hit if you were to back up. If it is clear, go to the back of the trailer, where the tandems are. Release the locking pins of the tandems by pulling/pushing the button or pulling out the release handle.

3. Get into the tractor and push in the YELLOW KNOB. Shift the tractor into REVERSE and back

the trailer until you feel and hear a bump sound, indicating that the tandems have slid to the front.

4. Pull out the YELLOW KNOB and shift the tractor into neutral.

5. Go to the back of the trailer, where the tandems are, and lock the locking pins by pushing/pulling the button or releasing the handle or pushing in the handle.

6. If the pins do not come back out, get in the tractor and rock the trailer by pushing in the YELLOW KNOB, then reverse, then go forward at least once. The tandem pins should lock; listen for the sound of them locking with the driver's side window down.

7. Pull out the YELLOW KNOB, and push in the RED KNOB. If you are leaving, push in BOTH KNOBS before driving off.

PROCEDURE FOR SLIDING TANDEMS TO THE BACK

You will need to slide the tandems to the back when getting live-loaded, live-unloaded, and after parking a trailer at the consignee where you will be dropping the trailer.

1. When you are in a safe area to slide the tandems, pull out BOTH KNOBS and make sure the tractor is in neutral.

2. Get out of the tractor, and go to the back of the trailer, where the tandems are, and release the locking pins of the tandems by pulling/pushing the button or pulling out the release handle.

3. Get into the tractor and push in the YELLOW KNOB. Shift the tractor into DRIVE (or forward gear for manual transmissions) and drive forward until you feel and hear a bump

Sliding Tandems | **63**

sound, indicating that the tandems have slid to the back.

4. Pull out the YELLOW KNOB and shift the tractor into neutral.

5. Go to the back of the trailer, where the tandems are, and lock the locking pins by pushing/pulling the button or releasing the handle or pushing in the handle.

6. If the pins do not come back out, get in the tractor and rock the trailer by pushing in the YELLOW KNOB, then reverse, then go forward at least once. The pins should lock; listen for the sound of them locking with the driver's side window down.

7. Pull out the YELLOW KNOB, and push in the RED KNOB. If you are leaving, push in BOTH KNOBS before driving off.

Note: some trailers/tractors are set up so that sliding the tandems can all be done inside the cab. Look in the tractor's factory manual, and contact your Driver Manager with regard to how to slide the tandems in this situation.

SECTION TEN
Maximum Weight Limits

It is necessary to ensure that the tractor-trailer you will be driving is within the legal weight limits. Bridges, roads, highways, and parking areas are only designed to hold so much weight. If tractor-trailers did not have legal weight limits, the maximum weight rating of a bridge could be exceeded and cause the bridge to collapse under all the weight.

There will be times where you will need to weigh the tractor-trailer at a CAT Scale to ensure none of the axles are above the legal maximum weight limits. Here are the maximum legal weight limits for tractor-trailers:

FRONT AXLE
12,000 pounds

DRIVE AXLES
34,000 pounds

TRAILER TANDEMS
34,000 pounds

GROSS (TOTAL)
80,000 pounds

    After you hook to a pre-loaded trailer or get live-loaded, you will receive the BOL (bill of lading, papers with the information of the load). On the BOL, the weight of the loaded trailer is documented. If the weight is 34,000 pounds or more, go to the nearest weigh scale and get weighed so you know if the tractor-trailer is within legal weight limits.

LEGAL DISCLAIMER: "Always weigh your truck and loads in accordance with your company's policies and DOT regulations. Never cause damage to any weigh scale. The author and Johnson Craftworks LLC relinquish liability."

Some shippers and receivers have weigh scales on their premises, but they do not always provide all four numbers. Most truck stops have a CAT Scale, which will provide all four numbers and a printed ticket inside the store available for you to pick up immediately after weighing.

Always send weigh tickets to the company you work for reimbursement. They may require you to mail the physical paper ticket, transflo (scan) the ticket, or send a digital copy of the ticket. Make sure to keep a copy for your personal records, and in case you are pulled over by DOT or law enforcement.

You can transflo the tickets inside a truck stop. Most truck stops have scanning devices for transfloing documents. Some truck companies have a phone application or scanning device inside the cab of the tractor which will allow you to scan and send the weigh tickets.

There is also a 'Weigh My Truck' phone app for use with CAT Scales. The app icon display the CAT Scale logo and name. Your employer will most likely approve the use of the app, but be sure to get weighed and send the weigh tickets according to the company's policy.

You will also need to add a payment method to the app and apply your desired setting prior to driving on a CAT Scale. A fee is charged through the app while getting weighed at the CAT Scale. Be sure to get the weigh tickets from inside the store, or send a digital copy of the weigh ticket to the company you drive for so you can receive reimbursement for the ticket fees.

If the load is over gross weight (+80,000 pounds), contact your Driver Manager for further instructions. You may be required to take the load back to the shipper so they can take weight off and issue updated BOLs with the new weight documented.

If you weigh the tractor-trailer and it is below 80,000 pounds but still above the legal weight limit on one or more of the axles, you will need to slide the tandems to adjust the axle weight. If after sliding the tandems a few times you are unable to get the axles at or below the legal weight limit, you will need to slide the 5th wheel to fine tune the weight distribution. If you do not know how to slide the 5th wheel, read chapter seven – "The 5th Wheel" in this guidebook.

NOTE: Fuel levels can affect the gross weight and weight distribution. It may be necessary to fuel first and weigh after to ensure that the tractor-trailer does not go over maximum weight limits after adding fuel to the fuel tank(s).

HOW TO USE A CAT SCALE

If you ever get a load that is 34,000 pounds or more (look for the weight on the BOL), go to the closest CAT Scale after leaving the shipper. CAT Scales can be found at most truck stops. Find a truck stop that has a CAT Scale as close to your current location as possible.

When you arrive at a CAT Scale and are ready to weigh, pull onto the scale. The front wheels need to be on the front plate, drive wheels on the middle plate, and the trailer wheels on the rear plate. SHIFT THE TRANSMISSION TO NEUTRAL AND PULL OUT THE YELLOW KNOB.

If you will not use the 'Weight My Truck' app, press the button on the call box. Follow the store clerk's instructions. If one or more of the axles are over the legal weight limit, you will need to find a safe place to park so you can slide the tandems and/or 5th wheel. After sliding the tandems and/or 5th wheel, return back to the CAT Scale, and weigh again. Do this as many times as necessary to get all the axles below the maximum weight limits. Don't forget to go inside and get the weigh tickets after you are finished.

If you are using the 'Weigh My Truck' app, open the app after parking on the CAT Scale and go through the process on the phone app. At the end, it will give you all four numbers. If all four are under the legal maximum weight, you can keep driving (don't forget to get the weigh ticket inside).

If one or more of the axles are above the maximum weight limit, you must find a safe area to park. After parking, you will need to slide the tandems and reweigh after. Do this as many times to get all four numbers under the maximum weight limits. You may also need to slide the 5th wheel to get the numbers under maximum weight limits. Make sure not to slide the 5th wheel too far forward, so that the tractor does not hit or damage the side of the trailer while making turns.

If you cannot get all four numbers under the maximum weight limits, you will need to contact your Driver Manager and inform them that the load is overweight. You may need to return to the shipper (if your Driver Manager says to do so) and have the shipper to take some stuff out the trailer to reduce weight. After that, you will need to reweigh again to ensure you are within the legal maximum weight limits. Don't forget to get the updated BOL after the shipper takes weight off.

OVERWEIGHT EXAMPLE

You hook to a loaded trailer at a shipper. Upon entering the checkout location, the security officer hand you the BOLs and check the seal on the back of the trailer. You notice on the BOLs, the weight is 41,500 pounds.

When you arrive to a CAT Scale at a nearby truck stop, the numbers are:

FRONT AXLE
11,000 pounds

DRIVE AXLES
30,000 pounds

TRAILER TANDEMS
36,000 pounds

GROSS (TOTAL)
77,000 pounds

    As you can see, the total weight of all the axles combined is okay at 77,000 pounds. The steer axle and drive axles are also okay, at 11,000 pounds and 30,000 pounds respectively. But the trailer tandems are 2,000 pounds overweight. You are required to slide the tandems to get the weight within legal limits.

    You park in a parking space at the truck stop with the hazards on, and slide the tandems toward the rear a few holes. You get back into the tractor and drive back onto the CAT Scale. The new numbers are:

FRONT AXLE
11,500 pounds

DRIVE AXLES
32,000 pounds

TRAILER TANDEMS
33,500 pounds

GROSS (TOTAL)
77,000 pounds

    All of the axles of the tractor-trailer are now below the maximum weight limits. You can now drive to deliver the load. Lorena pulled a 42,000-pound load right up a mountain without breaking a sweat! The total gross weight was about 79,000 pounds! Ha!

SECTION ELEVEN
Tractor-Trailers: Driving Forward

LEGAL DISCLAIMER: "Always follow the road rules, regulations, and road signs. Make turns and park so that the tractor and trailer do not collide with another vehicle, building, object, animal, or person. The author and Johnson Craftworks LLC relinquish liability."

"Never slow down on the interstate highway when taking an exit." an instructor said to one of their students. That same student happened to be someone I later had to train. When the student mentioned that to me, we were about to pass a rest area while driving down the interstate. "Look how short that exit ramp is to the rest area. If you wait to start slowing down until you are off the interstate, you won't have enough distance to brake in time. You would go in too fast and would lose control and drive off the ramp and into that ditch!"

I understand. It WOULD be dangerous to just slow down on the highway in theory. But I am not talking about slowing from 65 mph to 20 mph while still on the interstate though. That certainly WOULD be dangerous. But to clearly see how short an exit ramp is, and drive a tractor-trailer (which is a large, heavy vehicle that has long braking distances) full speed into the exit would be very foolish and dangerous.

Some exit ramps also are designed as a very tight bend, usually with signs posted that read 'Ramp, 25 MPH'. You certainly need to slow down early before approaching one of these types of exit ramps! They curve sharp, and usually a ditch is right off the asphalt! Imagine if there's water or ice on the pavement; you would definitely end up in that ditch!

Always pay attention to what is ahead of you when you are driving. Driving a tractor-trailer forward may seem easy and be similar to driving a car, but that could not be further from the truth. Speaking of forward driving... let's look at a few things that you should know about driving a tractor-trailer forward. I know it sound ridiculous, but you'll understand in a moment!

Due to the weight, size, length, and pivoting of tractor-trailers, it is common for new tractor-trailer drivers to make mistakes while driving forward. You have likely heard about backing incidents and new drivers struggling to perform an alley dock. But to be honest, driving a tractor-trailer forward can also prove to take necessary adjustments for new drivers. As a New Driver Trainer, I have seen student after student make certain mistakes while driving forward which could be very dangerous and costly for companies due to avoidable collisions and incidents.

PERSONAL EXAMPLES

I remember one time when I was a solo driver, and I went to make a turn at a particular intersection. I went as wide as I physically could without hitting anything, while turning into the road I wished to drive. I thankfully turned at a slow enough speed, and also checked the driver side mirror a few times to look at the back of the trailer. I immediately hit the brakes and stopped.

There was a car on the inside of the turn that drove up to the light too far. If I had not stopped, the trailer would have hit the car. There was only a few feet of space between the back of the trailer and the car. Even after turning as wide as I could, I still needed to look into the mirror to see where the trailer was, and if I was going to hit anything on the inside of the turn. That one thing, looking into the mirror to check if I had enough space to clear the turn, is what saved me from hitting that car and possibly getting fired and losing the company money.

It happened another time, while driving onboard with the person who was my driver mentor. I was exiting a particular place, and the place had a cement block on the inside of the turn. I did not turn wide enough, and the trailer would have hit the cement block on the inside of the turn. I saw it in the mirror and stopped the truck before I could hit it. I reversed the truck and then turned wide when I drove forward again, and was able to complete the turn without hitting the cement block. Going wide while turning is important when driving a tractor-trailer.

STUDENT EXAMPLES

On a particular interstate exit ramp, I noticed the design of the ramp and overhead bridge. It created a severe blind spot while going around the exit ramp. At the time, one of my students was driving. "If you are driving and approaching a corner where you can't see what is around the corner, you need to reduce your speed and mentally prepare to stop." I told my student.

The student said "Okay" and slowed down the truck. After turning into the exit ramp, all of a sudden, we were met with cars and trucks in both lanes which were stopped. There was an incident further up the exit ramp, and the road was temporarily blocked off so that the damaged vehicles and parts could be removed from the road. My student was able to slow down in time and stop without hitting the back of the stopped vehicles. That was a close call! And right on time for the lesson I gave the student!

In a different situation, one of my students went to make a right turn. This was a few days into training, and I had said and explained multiple times the necessity of checking the trailer in the mirrors while turning. This particular time, I noticed the student wasn't checking the mirrors while making the turn. I knew ahead of time that they were going to hit a light pole on the inside of the turn if they kept driving forward.

"Look in the mirror, you'll hit that light pole if you keep going forward! Hit the brakes!" Immediately, they stopped and then looked in the mirror. "Do you see why it's important to look in the mirror to check the clearance of the trailer and objects on the inside of the turn?"

A particular student I was training had an issue with parking. Most of us have went years, even decades parking smaller cars and trucks with no trailer hooked. It may sound ridiculous, but even parking a tractor-trailer while driving forward can be an issue for new drivers. It's the fact that trailers (especially long trailers) off-track from the turning radius and location of the tractor.

This cause a common issue with new tractor-trailer drivers when driving forward into parking spaces. The tractor will be in the middle of the parking space, but the trailer will be off in the parking space next over. This come from turning too early and from too close a distance from the parking space. This particular student also could not correct the mistake while backing due to turning the steering wheel too much or in the wrong direction and still ending up crooked.

DRIVING FORWARD: ACCOUNTING FOR THE TRAILER

A great deal of focus with new tractor-trailer drivers is with regard to backing. This is a good thing. But I have realized that a driver's backing is only as good as their forward driving. By default, if their forward driving is not readjusted to account for having a trailer hooked, they will not develop the necessary 'trailer conscious' needed to perform backing maneuvers with a sense of control and purposeful direction.

As I say with regard to tractor-trailer drivers, "Always go wide" when making turns, or attempting to park forward (which is called a 'pull-through') into a parking space.

Don't be aggressive with it, never attempt to turn so wide that you risk hitting something with the front of the truck, or with the front of the trailer.

When you are making a turn, the trailer on the front sticks out, and the trailer could hit something if you attempt to turn too wide and get too close to other trucks, trailers, buildings, or objects. Only turn as wide as you need to complete a turn or pull-through without hitting anything on the inside or outside of the turn.

Hitting curbs cost truck companies money. Each time a curb is hit, the tires accumulate damage to their structure and material. Over time, the risk of a tire blowout or failure increase. While performing pre-trip inspections on the trailers I hook to, I can tell if the tires have had contact with curbs and other objects. The damage can be obvious and severe if the same tires have struck curbs by the same driver or multiple drivers. Tires for tractor-trailers are expensive, and the more you hit curbs, the more money it cost the company you drive for to replace those tires when they blow or fail.

It is also important to check the mirror of the direction you are turning. If you are making a right turn, check the RIGHT mirror and look at the trailer and the tandems to ensure you are not about to hit something. If you are making a left turn, check the LEFT mirror and look at the trailer and the tandems to ensure you are not about to hit something. Whatever direction you turn, LOOK in that mirror and at the trailer.

5TH WHEEL AND TANDEMS LOCATION

Forward driving also 'feels' different depending on the location of the tandems and 5th wheel. If the tandems and 5th wheel are all the way forward (toward the tractor's engine) it may feel as if turns are easier, and you have more space to make turns and perform backing maneuvers. The issue though, is that if the load is too heavy, you will need to slide the tandems toward the rear some amount so that all the axles are below the maximum weight limits.

If the 5th wheel is all the way to the front, the tractor could hit the side of the trailer (depending on the design of the tractor and what type of trailer is hooked). The airlines and electrical cable also might hang too low and drag on the catwalk or catch on something and be pulled from the glad hand connections.

If the tandems and 5th wheel are all the way to the back, it will feel like you need a lot of space to make turns and perform backing maneuvers. It will seem difficult to make turns wide enough to not hit curbs and objects on the inside of the turn. The airlines and electrical cable also need to stretch longer to account for the extra space between the tractor and trailer.

While making turns, the airlines and electrical cable also need to stretch further. This might require an additional hangar, or the original hangar to be adjusted to suit the extra space between the tractor and trailer.

Hazard lights are a useful way to communicate your intention or hazard to other drivers. While driving mountains and parking forward, use the hazard lights to communicate (broken down, attempting to pull-through park, ascending and descending mountains, ext.). This can lower collisions and fatalities between drivers, parked vehicles, and people walking or standing in the area. Use the city horn if necessary to alert pedestrians and people walking or standing nearby when attempting to pull-through park.

While ascending mountains, you might see that black flatbed tractor-trailer behind you. If you are in the right lane with the hazard lights on, they will know to change lanes to safely pass on the left. You may also be walking from your truck to the bathroom of a rest area and hear a city horn blow. Oh! There's that flatbed!

SECTION TWELVE
Backing Maneuvers: The Pentaplex

Backing a tractor-trailer well is a necessity for Class A CDL drivers. But it prove to be difficult for many new drivers, and a major cause of collisions and incidents. Backing – not just a maneuver, but the ultimate challenge of your driving skill.

All truck driving schools will teach backing maneuvers, but not all will teach the ones which will be necessary for the duties you will perform on the job. We will look at the five maneuvers I find to be important to know how to perform well. Although two of these maneuvers are not 'backing' maneuvers, they are maneuvers you will perform while driving for any company you work for. I firmly think all truck schools should teach these five maneuvers.

We are going to take a look at the pull-through, U-turn, straight-line back, alley dock, and dock-offset. I call this the 'pentaplex'.

The dock-offset is a refined version of the 'offset back'. The offset back, as it is traditionally taught in trucking schools, is incorrect for specific reasons which will be described later in this chapter.

NOTES ON PERFORMING BACKING MANEUVERS

While performing any of these maneuvers, you will need to check the side mirrors to ensure you will not hit anything. Although you will have your head out the window and looking back while performing an alley dock and dock-offset, you still need to occasionally check the passenger side mirror.

The 'primary mirror' is the mirror you will check the most, and the 'occasional mirror' is the mirror you will check occasionally. The primary mirror will usually be the driver side mirror. If you are performing a blind side alley dock (which I never recommend), the passenger mirror will become the primary mirror'.

NOTE ON BLIND SIDE BACKING: Although I recommend to never blind side back, there are truck stops and rarely a shipper where the only way to back into a particular space is to blind side back. If you must blind side back, you are required to get out and look. Never perform a blind side back by chance or hope. Always use the mirrors and get out and look to ensure you will not hit anything.

G.O.A.L. stands for 'Get Out And Look'. While performing backing maneuvers, it is recommended that you get out and look at least one time to ensure that you will not hit anything if you were to continue to back. Still, until this day, I personally get out and look. There is no shame in the G.O.A.L.!

Trailer Action – this is the motion of the tractor-trailer increasing the degree of angle while backing, even if the steering wheels are straight. This is called 'trailer action', and it is wise to back in a manner which account for this.

While performing a straight-line back, you may have to turn the wheel to make adjustments so that the trailer will go in the direction you desire. Whenever the tractor-trailer has an angle, it will create a blind spot in one of the mirrors in which you are no longer able to see what is behind the trailer in that particular mirror. If you straighten the truck and trailer temporarily, you will be able to look in both mirrors to see what is behind you before continuing to back.

Always pull forward if you are backing and you see that you will hit something if you were to continue to back.

There is no shame in the pull up! Always pull forward with the steer wheels straight and make your adjustments while going back. Use all the space in front of the truck when pulling forward.

Then, while backing, make the necessary adjustments to direct the trailer in the direction you desire. While performing an alley dock or a dock-offset, pull forward with the steer wheels straight. Then make your corrections while going back. When making your corrections going back, use small adjustments to the steering; there is no need to turn the steering wheel a lot. Only turn the steer wheels as much as you need.

Backing also 'feels' different depending on the location of the tandems and 5th wheel. You may find yourself needing more space to back if the tandems and 5th wheel are all the way to the back. You may find yourself needing to add a lot of angle while backing with the tandems and 5th wheel all the way to the back. Backing will feel easier if the tandems and 5th wheel are further up (towards the tractor's engine).

LEGAL DISCLAIMER: "Always perform backing and forward maneuvers according to the policies of the company you drive for, and recommendations given by your Driver Manager. Never back in a manner that could cause a collision with another vehicle, object, building, animal, or person. The author and Johnson Craftworks LLC relinquish liability."

THE PULL-THROUGH

I know it sound ridiculous, but parking a tractor-trailer while driving forward isn't as easy as it sounds. I constantly see the same thing at truck stops and rest areas when trucks drive forward into a parking space. The tractor will be perfectly in the middle of the parking space, but the trailer will be over into the parking space next over. Or the trailer will be in the parking space, but it will be crooked and make it difficult for a truck to park in the space next over.

The pull-through is basically attempting to park in a parking space while driving forward. Some truck stops and most rest areas are designed so that trucks don't have to back into some of the parking spaces. If you perform a pull-through, ensure that you are far enough away from the parking space and go wide before turning. If you are too close to the parking space, when you turn into the space, you will find that the trailer is crooked, or in the parking space next over.

If you pull-through and the trailer is crooked, rather than backing, pull forward with the wheels straight. As you pull forward, the trailer will slowly line up with the tractor and parallel with the parking space. If it is still crooked after you pull forward straight, perform a straight-line back, only using small adjustments to the steering to align the tractor and trailer with the parking space. Remember, when performing a straight-line back, a small adjustment equal a big movement.

THE U-TURN

Why would a U-turn be difficult in a tractor-trailer? Well, U-turns ARE easy! But a common issue new drivers experience when making U-turns in a tractor-trailer is that they turn too much. The airlines and electrical cable will pull from the glad hand connections, or the back side of the tractor will hit the trailer and cause damage. This is the result of turning the steer wheels all the way, and not paying attention to the angle of the tractor and trailer.

When performing a U-turn, the angle of the tractor-trailer should never exceed 85 degrees. An angle greater than 85 degrees is called a 'jackknife'. Jackknifing is unnecessary and should never happen while operating a tractor-trailer. Jackknifing is a driving error, not an issue with the tractor-trailer.

There will be times when you will need to perform a U-turn at a truck stop, shipper, or receiver. When getting ready to perform a U-turn, go really slow, then turn the steering wheel all the way in the direction you wish to go. You will need to look into the mirrors and at the angle of the tractor-trailer. When you are getting close to 75 to 80 degrees, start turning the wheel in the opposite direction to keep the tractor-trailer form increasing in angle. This will prevent you from jackknifing the tractor-trailer.

Do not perform a U-turn at a high speed. Doing so create a wide turning radius, meaning you will need a lot of room to complete the U-turn. Perform the U-turn in a safe location, and at a low speed. 5 MPH is more than enough.

While performing a U-turn, ensure that you do not hit anything with the front of the truck, inside the U-turn area, and with the front of the trailer on the opposite side. The front of the trailer will stick out far when performing a U-turn. Also, never perform a U-turn in the highway or road.

STRAIGHT-LINE BACK

The straight-line back is the foundation of backing a tractor-trailer. If you are unable to perform a straight-line back without hitting things (cones, barriers, ext.), or not maintaining control of the trailer, you will need to perfect this backing maneuver. All other backing maneuvers will be finished with a straight-line back. It is a must that you can perform a straight-line back well.

Use both mirrors while backing. Your primary mirror to check will be the driver side mirror. Occasionally check the passenger side mirror to ensure you will not hit anything and the trailer is not going in a direction you don't want it to go.

Small adjustment = big movement. A good straight-line back does not require much steering. You will find that smooth and small adjustments to the steering keep the trailer in a straight line.

If you will need to dock the trailer, do not ram the dock. Back slowly and gently bump the dock. If you will back where there is a curb behind the trailer, do not back until you hit the curb. The tires could pinch the mudflaps on the tandems and rip them off! If you are backing where there is a barricade behind the trailer, do not ram the barricade with the trailer. Get the bumper of the trailer close to the barricade and then park.

ALLEY DOCK (SET-UP AND BEND)

I know you are probably thinking "Did he skip or forget about the offset backing maneuver?" I certainly have not forgotten! Remember earlier I mentioned that offset backing as it is taught in trucking schools is incorrect. I will explain why later in this chapter. But to perform an offset back (I call it the dock-offset) the correct way, it is necessary that you can perform an alley dock well.

"Turn the wheels hard right then go back. Okay, stop! Now, turn the wheels hard left and go back." one trucking school instructor said to one of their students. It is a wonder how ridiculous all the measurements, hard turning, and specific distances school instructors teach their students to perform an alley dock.

The issue is that in the real world, you will not always be able to drive the truck a specific amount of distance from the parking space, be able to turn the wheels all the way (due to limited space), and back a specific distance in certain locations. There has to be a simpler and more efficient way to learn and perform an alley dock which work 100% of the time, and I will share that method with you below!

NOTE: Only turn 'hard right' or 'hard left' if you absolutely need to. Remember trailer action? If you turn the wheels hard right or left, you will have too much angle, and risk jackknifing. You only need to turn the wheels as much as you need to get the trailer to go in the direction you desire.

Always bend the trailer outside the parking space, and never inside the parking space. If you attempt to bend the trailer inside the parking space, you could hit the truck or trailer in the parking space next over.

NOTE: You are required to roll down the driver side window, stick your head out the window and look directly at the trailer whenever you perform an alley dock. Depending on the mirror design, only using the mirrors could cause you to misjudge the spacing and distance between your trailer and other things (buildings, other trailers, tractors, ext.). Always stick your head out the driver side window and look directly at the back of your trailer and what is behind the trailer.

There are only two things to perform in order to master the alley dock. They are the 'Set-up' and the 'Bend'. I call this the Set-up & Bend. Alley dock can be mistaught easily by having too many steps or not understanding that no two alley docks will ever be the same. To simplify the process, I only teach two steps, and that is the set-up and the bend. By simplifying the process, an alley dock can be performed anywhere, regardless of available space.

ALLEY DOCK: THE SET-UP

The only important thing to remember about the set-up, it is to simply position the tractor-trailer in a way that will allow you to perform an alley dock without hitting anything or using excessive pull-ups (and hard steering).

ALLEY DOCK: THE BEND

After you set up, the only thing that is left is to back and manage the bend (angle) of the tractor-trailer so that you can park the trailer in the desired parking space. You have only two options when doing an alley dock, and that is to turn the steering wheel to either add bend or take bend away. You only need enough bend to direct the trailer into the parking space.

Having too much bend will cause the trailer to miss the parking space and go too close to the inside. Having too little bend will cause the trailer to miss the parking space and go too far to the outside. Managing the bend (by adding or taking away) will direct the trailer where you want it to go. Be mindful which direction you will need to turn the steering wheel to add or take bend away.

DOCK-OFFSET

Offset backing as taught in truck schools pose various problems in the real world. The main issue is that you will not always have enough space to drive so far ahead, and then back into the parking space next over. Many truck stops and shipper locations physically are not designed with the traditional offset backing maneuver in mind.

Another issue is that offset backing as it is taught in trucking schools, require excessive use of the side mirrors, too much steering, and backing on the blind side. This is inconsistent, as tractors have different sized and angled mirrors. Tractors also have different steering ratios and turning radiuses. The way you perform an offset back in one tractor would feel and be different than the next tractor.

Here is a different, easier, and more efficient method of performing an offset back. I call it the dock-offset.

In its simplest form, the dock-offset is just performing an alley dock into the other parking space. Just pull out the space and drive to the left and do an alley dock into the other parking space. But it is necessary to be able to perform an alley dock well to perform a dock-offset.

LEFT SIDE DOCK-OFFSET: If you are in a parking space and wish to dock-offset to your left, pull out of the parking space and turn left, and set up as if you are going to do an alley dock. Then perform an alley dock into the parking space to the left. You may need to pull forward a little further than you usually would. You may need to add a little more bend than you think you need to back into the space.

RIGHT SIDE DOCK-OFFSET: If you are in a parking space and wish to dock-offset to your right, pull out of the parking space and turn left, and set up as if you are going to do an alley dock. Then perform an alley dock into the parking space to the right. You may need to take away some bend to back into the space.

THE JACKKNIFE

At no time should you ever jackknife a tractor-trailer. Jackknifing is when the tractor-trailer is at a 90-degree angle or more. Jackknifing is unnecessary and could cause damage to the airlines and electrical cable, and could damage the side of the tractor or trailer. If you are in a situation where you need a lot of bend to rotate the trailer some amount, never exceed an 85-degree angle. It would be more favorable to reposition the truck, then back where so much angle isn't required.

THE 45 BACK

It may seem like the 45 back is easier and more simple to perform than an alley dock. But know that more space is required to perform a 45 back. Due to the angle of a 45 being in between 90 and 0, when backing, it will be difficult to see the back of the trailer while your head is out the window, but then if you look in the mirror while adding bend, you can't see much of the trailer and the parking space. It may help to have the tandems closer to the parking space when setting up to perform a 45 back than you would an alley dock. Always get out and look when performing a 45 back.

BONUS BACKING MANEUVER: THE SWINGSIDE BACK

There was a particular location where the designated parking spot I was instructed to drop the trailer was in a difficult to reach area. The parking space was at the end of a row of trailers. A building blocked the way. There was also a row of trailers on the opposite side, so there was not enough room to pull into an empty parking space to straight-line back.

I sat in the seat looking at the situation and thought if only I could somehow position the trailer so that the tail of the trailer was aimed at the parking space, I could back into it. Then I realized if I drove forward on the right side of the row of trailers leading to the parking space, I could do a U-turn in front of the parking space. As I would do the U-turn, the tail end of the trailer would eventually point toward the parking space. From there I could alley dock into the parking space.

I attempted the maneuver and was able to back the trailer into the parking space. What I did was combine the U-turn maneuver and the alley dock maneuver into a single maneuver. I called it the 'Swingside Back'.

I love this backing maneuver, because it is also useful to prevent the need of blind side backing. You will have to get close to the trailers (or trucks) all the way to the right. Once your tractor is in front of the parking space, you will turn the wheels all the way to the left to perform a left side U-turn. DO NOT jackknife the tractor-trailer. Do not drive at a high speed while performing the U-turn. 5 MPH is more than enough.

As the bend of the tractor-trailer increase, you will notice that the tail end of the trailer will aim at different parking spots as it rotate. Once the tail end of the trailer just pass the empty space you wish to back into, then you can stop and do an alley dock into the parking space. Remember to roll the window down so that you can look at the back of the trailer. Use the driver side mirror to ensure you do not jackknife the trailer.

RECOMMENDATIONS FOR BACKING MANEUVERS

- ✓ When performing an alley dock or dock-offset (and you are positioned and ready to back), roll down the driver side window and stick your head out the window so you can directly see where the trailer is going as you back and manage bend.

- ✘ NEVER use your mirrors only while doing an alley dock. Check both mirrors. Check the passenger side mirror occasionally to ensure you are not going to hit something.

- ✓ SLOWLY add bend as you are backing and do not turn the steering wheel quickly or too much. You will end up adding too much bend too soon by turning the steering wheel quickly.

- ✘ NEVER jackknife (90-degree angle or more) the tractor-trailer while doing an alley dock.

- ✓ While performing an alley dock or dock-offset, you will notice the angle of the tractor-trailer increase as you back. You will eventually need to turn the steering wheel the opposite way to keep the angle from increasing more than you need.

- ✘ NEVER bend (rotate) the trailer inside the parking space. Bend the tractor-trailer outside the parking space so that you don't risk hitting a truck or trailer that is next to the parking space you are backing into.

✓ Turn on back lights when reversing a bobtail at night for extra lighting.

SECTION THIRTEEN
Trailer Load & Unload

You learned earlier in this guidebook about hooking and dropping trailers, whether they are empty or loaded. In this chapter we will look at the loading and unloading of trailers specifically. It is necessary for the trailer door(s) to be open for a live or dock load/unload. Certain locations (ex. food processing facilities) may require you to dock with the door(s) closed, unless otherwise instructed.

LEGAL DISCLAIMER: "Always follow the instructions of the shipper, receiver, the company you drive for, and your Driver Manager with regard to docking, undocking, loading, and unloading of trailers. The author and Johnson Craftworks LLC relinquish liability."

Some shippers and receivers can be picky about the cleanliness of the trailer. Reefers require cleaning and washouts of the trailer before each live load and dock load. Truck wash and trailer washouts will be discussed in chapter 15 - 'The Bread & Butter' of this guidebook.

You may have to sweep out the trailer before going to get live loaded or drop loaded. Sweep out trailers in a legal location and dispose of the trash in a trash can or dumpster. Never sweep trash and debris from trailers onto the road or driveway.

NOTES ON LOAD AND UNLOAD

When you arrive at a shipper or consignee, you will be given instruction on where to dock and how. Some locations will verbally provide the instructions, others will hand you a paper with instructions on where and how to dock. Some locations have a buzzer device which will alert you what door number to go to. The buzzer will also indicate when they are ready to live load/unload your trailer and when they are finished live loading/unloading.

The shipper will provide the BOL (Bill of Lading) to you either once you arrive and check in, or after you are finished getting loaded. The consignee will sign the BOLs upon arrival. Sometimes they may require you to get unloaded first before they hand you the signed BOLs back.

Most shippers and receivers will require you to open the trailer door(s) and slide the tandems to the rear before you dock the trailer. Most docks will have a green light and red light, others will have a single light which can switch between green and red. Some locations might not have any lights at all, and someone will knock on your truck door with the BOLs when the live load or unload is finished.

At lighted docks, the light will start off green. After you dock the trailer, the light will turn red, indicating that the live loading or unloading process has begun. You will have to wait until the light turn green again to be able to pull the trailer from the dock.

LEGAL DISCLAIMER: "Always follow the instructions of the shippers and receivers with regard to docking and undocking trailers. Never pull a trailer from a dock when the light is red. Never pull a trailer from a dock when you are not authorized to do so. The author and Johnson Craftworks LLC relinquish liability."

Note: live load and live unload could take 10 minutes or hours. It is never a specific time.

LIVE LOAD

Different than hooking to a preloaded trailer, a live load is when you dock an empty trailer, and the trailer is loaded while you are hooked to it. You will wait for the trailer to finish being loaded before being able to pull the trailer from the dock.

LIVE UNLOAD

Similar to a live load, instead, the trailer will be unloaded while it is docked, and you are still hooked to it. You will wait for the trailer to finish being unloaded before being able to pull the trailer from the dock.

DOCK LOAD (DOCK AND DROP)

A dock load (aka dock and drop) is docking an empty trailer and dropping it while it is docked. The trailer is then loaded while you are free to bobtail to pick up a new trailer. Some shippers will have you dock drop and park your bobtail in front of the trailer while it is being loaded, or park in a different location on the premises. Once the trailer is finished being loaded, you will be notified (usually a phone call, text, shipping clerk, or buzzer device) to re-hook to the now loaded trailer.

DOCK UNLOAD (DOCK AND DROP)

A dock unload (aka dock and drop) is docking a loaded trailer and dropping it while it is docked. The trailer is then unloaded while you are free to bobtail to pick up a new trailer. Some receivers will have you dock drop and park your bobtail in front of the trailer while it is being unloaded, or park in a different location on the premises. Once the trailer is finished being unloaded, you will be notified (usually a phone call, text, shipping clerk, or buzzer device) to re-hook to the now empty trailer.

There's that flatbed! Flatbed trailers can be loaded nearly anywhere. You'll typically see them at construction sites and getting loaded without having to be docked. Loading and unloading of flatbeds will not be discussed in this guidebook.

SECTION FOURTEEN
Mountain Driving

It was a particular student I was training. For some reason, the student would get anxious and panic whenever the truck would go down a short hill or mountain. Tractor-trailers are large and heavy, so they definitely will slow down some while going up a hill, and speed up some while going down a hill.

The student could not tell whether they were going downhill or uphill. To them, the truck was always on flat ground, and somehow would begin speeding up or slowing down on its own. Mountain driving proved worse for this particular student.

While going down mountains and steep downgrades, the student wasn't able to tell why the truck would all of a sudden begin speeding up, and the student would wait until the truck was going too fast to then try and get it under control. By that point it is too late. I had to always notify this particular student whenever a downgrade was approaching so that they could do the necessary preparations ahead of time.

This also deemed to be problematic, as the student had a tendency to ride the foot brake rather than use the engine break. I found all of this to be too dangerous, so I chose to not allow this particular student to continue the training and hiring process. I potentially saved a life, and the lives of others.

This is a huge issue and danger for new tractor-trailer drivers. Driving a small car or truck down or up a hill or mountain is a lot different than a large, heavy tractor-trailer. There are necessary adjustments that need to be made.

THE REALITY OF MOUNTAIN DRIVING

Face your fears – they are the gatekeepers to greater joy and success. Mountain driving may sound scary at first, but with the right training and preparations, it is not as scary as you think. Those who put aside their fears and learn how to drive tractor-trailers around mountains, are able to see some beautiful sights.

This is especially true when at the top of a mountain and descending, you are able to look down at the Earth from high up. Its life changing, in a good way. As said earlier, tractor-trailer driving is not just a job, but an experience. It is a life changing experience.

Below we will look at some safe mountain driving practices, and a four-step procedure for descending mountains that will keep you safe and the truck under your control. Always have the hazard lights on and drive in the right lane when climbing and descending mountains and steep downgrades.

LEGAL DISCLAIMER: "Always follow the policies and procedures for mountain driving in accordance with the company you drive for, your Driver Manager's recommendations, and DOT laws. The author and Johnson Craftworks LLC relinquish liability."

CLIMBING MOUNTAINS

Climbing a mountain is more simple than descending a mountain. When going up mountains and steep inclines, get into the far-right lane and turn on the hazard lights. Keep up your momentum; the truck will slow down as it go up the mountain (or steep incline). Keep your foot on the fuel pedal all the way up the incline if you are not driving on cruise control. If you are driving on cruise control, the cruise control will keep the truck up the hill or incline, although it will still slow some.

If you are driving a manual transmission, you may have to downshift while climbing, as the truck could lose a lot of speed and the tractor's engine revs could drop too low. It is recommended to reduce your speed and downshift before climbing, so that you do not have to downshift while going up the incline. In all-electric tractors, keep on the power pedal, or if you are driving on cruise control, the cruise control will keep you up the incline.

If you come to a truck ahead of you that is moving slower, make a pass if it is safe to do so. Get back into the right lane after making the pass.

DESCENDING MOUNTAINS

I remember the first time I climbed and descended a mountain. Going up, I changed into the right lane and put on the hazard lights. The truck slowed to about 40 mph. I looked in the driver side mirror and saw a train of trucks behind me, all in the right lane with their hazard lights on. I was leading the pack! Literally, there were about a dozen trucks following behind me.

At the top, due to my truck having a speed limiter, some of the other trucks passed me. But while going down the same mountain, I changed into the right lane again, with the hazard lights on. I fronted another pack of trucks, all behind me with their hazard lights on. That surely was hilarious to me, and an experience I'll never forget!

If you will be driving interstate to interstate, there will eventually come a time you will have to descend a mountain or steep downgrade. If you are driving and find yourself going up an incline or mountain, eventually you will have to go down the mountain. Usually there will be a sign or two ahead of time before you come to a downgrade. Here are some examples of the signs you might see:

"TRUCKS USE LOW GEAR"
"DOWNGRADE NEXT 5 MILES"

"6% DOWNGRADE NEXT 3 MILES"

There may be a picture of a truck going downgrade. There may be no sign at all. Always pay attention to the road and surroundings incase a downgrade is coming but there are no signs on the road.

NOTE: Always use the right lane with the hazard lights on when descending mountains and steep downgrades.

If you are unsure how to safely descend a mountain or downgrade, or do not have a procedure to follow, this is the procedure I personally use and teach my students.

BASIC PROCEDURE FOR DESCENDING MOUNTAINS

1. **TURN ON HAZARD LIGHTS** – You will be reducing your speed and don't want traffic behind you to run into the back of you! GET INTO THE RIGHT LANE and turn on the hazard lights so that other vehicles can change into a different lane and make a safe pass around you.

2. **BRAKE TO 40 MPH** – bring your speed and momentum down, before going down the mountain. DO NOT wait to slow down while you are already descending. Slow down BEFORE descending.

3. **SET CRUISE CONTROL TO 40 MPH** – The engine brake can be strong. You don't want to set the engine brake and it slow down the truck too much to where you are going too slow. The cruise control is set to keep the truck from slowing down too much. If you slow down too much, vehicles and trucks behind you may not be able to brake in time or see you after they come around a corner to avoid running into the back of you.

4. **SET ENGINE BRAKE TO MODERATE SETTING** – The final step is to set the engine brake

to a moderate setting. Do not crank the engine brake to maximum. Only use the amount of engine brake you need to keep from speeding up while descending.

Once you reach the bottom of the mountain or downgrade, turn off the engine brake and hazard lights and accelerate back up to speed. Never exceed the speed limit while descending mountains and downgrades. Never exceed the speed limit after reaching the bottom of a downgrade or mountain.

Not all downgrades are steep enough to necessitate slowing down to 40 mph. You will still have to use some amount of engine brake (or exhaust, or electronic brake), but with no cruise control.

If Lorena can keep a 42,000-pound load from losing control down a mountain, surely with the right preparations, you can maintain control of the truck you are driving while descending a steep downgrade.

ENGINE BRAKE, NOT FOOT BRAKE!

- Stay off the foot brake and use the engine brake (or exhaust or electronic brake on some tractors)

- DO NOT use the foot brake going down mountains as your primary means to keep the truck from speeding up. The brakes will overheat and fade if you do this!

- Reduce your speed, and set the engine brake to a moderate setting BEFORE going down the mountain, and only use the foot brake as a supplement to keep the truck from speeding up on very steep downgrades. Never ride the foot brake.

- DO NOT go down the mountain at high speed and then wait until the truck is going fast to use the engine brake! You would end up fighting against the truck to slow it down. You must slow down and set the engine brake BEFORE going down.

STRAIGHT TIMED BRAKING

On very steep downgrades, it is possible that the engine brake set to a high level while descending at a low speed will not be enough to keep the truck from speeding up. Some downgrades may be too steep for the load weight you are pulling. You will have to use the foot brake as a supplement to the engine brake.

    The important thing about Straight Timed Braking, is that you are never riding the foot brake. You are only stepping on the foot brake while the truck is going straight and not in a curve or turn. You are only stepping on the brake for short, timed intervals to slow the truck. You must brake hard, and not gently.

    On very steep downgrades where a low speed and high engine brake setting is not enough, you will need to perform the four steps listed above at a low but safe speed. You will have to perform the four steps, along with the Straight Timed Braking added as a fifth step.

SECTION FIFTEEN
The Bread & Butter

There are a lot more things that are not covered in CDL manuals or at trucking schools than just weigh stations and using an ELD. Much of your work and time out on the road won't consist of performing an alley dock or doing a pre-trip inspection. Although those two things are important to perform well, still most of your day will consist of other activities. Let's take a quick look at these activities that will fill your days out on the road.

HANDS-FREE DEVICES

While you are driving and away from home, you will want to remain in contact with family and loved ones. Your Driver Manager or Dispatcher will also need to contact you from time to time. Hands-free wireless devices and headsets are very useful tools that allow you to keep your hands on the steering wheel and eyes on the road, while communicating when it is necessary.

Most truck stops will have headsets and hands-free devices for sale. You can also find them online at discounted prices. Purchasing a hands-free device or headset from a truck stop may be a better option for those who don't have online accounts or would prefer to shop in a physical store.

Make sure to purchase one that will connect and work with your mobile phone or device, and that it has important features such as noise cancelation and button operated power and volume options.

There may come a time where 'flesh embedded' or 'bone-fused' communication devices supplement or replace the typical hands-free devices we are used to seeing. These flesh embedded (or bone-fused) devices would be used to receive and make phone calls, without the need for ever touching a button or screen. These flesh embedded devices would only require voice activation, meaning your hands stay on the steering wheel and eyes on the road, even while making or receiving a phone call.

DISPATCHED ON LOADS

Your Driver Manager or Dispatch will be in charge of dispatching you on loads to pick up and deliver. Each company will have their own process for loads, but generally you will receive load assignments on the ELD, which will have all the information you will need to know.

Information such as the pickup location, load ID number, pickup time, fuel stops, and drop off location will be included in the load assignment. You will have to time manage the loads yourself to ensure they are delivered on time. If you are unable to take certain types of loads for whatever reason, you will need to discuss that with your Driver Manager.

Your Dispatcher will keep you driving. Truck companies want to make profit and lots of it. If the trucks don't keep moving with loads attached, the companies will be in a negative financial balance by default (due to insurance, contract subscriptions, running costs, property taxes, ext.). The trucking industry is ALWAYS busy. There is always an abundance of work, and your Driver Manager will keep you busy.

The more truck companies can keep their trucks moving and loads delivered, the more money they make. That relates to potentially more you can earn through bonuses, promotions, more miles (or hours), and other incentives. Keep your Driver Manager happy and they will keep you driving.

ROUTES

Know whether you will be driving intrastate (within the same state), interstate (from one state to another), local (within a city or town), over the road (aka OTR, interstate), regional (specific side of the country), or dedicated (usually contracted loads delivering to same locations). They are not all the same and pay will be different. If you need to be home on weekends, want to drive interstate and travel while making money, or want to be home every night, these are things to consider.

NAVIGATION

There are things (and sometimes people) which you hate and love at the same time. Many truck drivers complain about that ol' ELD that is installed in most tractors. It could be the fact that it lags a few minutes behind whenever messages are sent to it, or the navigation freeze while driving, causing you to miss exits or make wrong turns.

It could be that the navigation is outdated, never upgraded with modern maps, and will not show truck stops, rest areas, fueling stations, charging stations (for all-electric tractors), and truck wash centers. Sometimes it will malfunction and shut off while you are driving and take a long time to power up when it has been off for a while.

Many truck drivers use separate navigation systems. They can be purchased at truck stops, purchased online, and delivered to your doorstep, or downloaded on your mobile phone or device. The important thing to note is that whatever navigation you use, it must be designed specifically for tractor-trailers.

Class A Commercial Motor Vehicles are large and heavy. The navigation must guide you away from bridges that are too low to pass, roads, and bridges with weight limits too low, streets and roadways which prohibit large/heavy vehicles, and dead ends where you will be unable to perform a U-turn.

Two common navigations that many truck drivers use are the phone apps called 'Trucker Path: Truck GPS & Maps' as well as 'Hammer: Truck GPS & Maps'. They can be downloaded in the app store on your phone or tablet. Personally, I only use the Trucker Path phone app. I find it far superior to the navigation on the ELD.

TRANSFLO BOLS (GET PAID)

Any time you pick up a load whether it is a preloaded trailer, or you will get live loaded, you will receive BOLs from the shipper. BOLs are paperwork for the load you will deliver. You must take and keep the BOLs with you all the way to the consignee (receiving location). Always sign your name on the BOLs where it is indicated as 'Carrier Signature' or 'Driver Signature'.

After you have delivered the load, the consignee will sign the BOLs and give you one of them back with their signature (or a receiving stamp). You will have to send that to the company you drive for. Owner operators may follow a different process. Transflo devices are found at most truck stops. You go into the truck stop and follow the process as instructed by the facility to scan the paperwork to send to the company you drive for.

Your company may also have a mobile phone app for scanning and sending the BOLs digitally. There may also be a scanning device located inside the cab of the tractor. Always follow the instructions for scanning and sending paperwork as outlined by the company you drive for.

FUELING & CHARGING

The load won't move if the truck has no fuel (or power for CEVs). Most truck stops have fuel isles. At the fuel isles, there are diesel pumps on both sides, usually a DEF pump on the driver side, trash cans, and water buckets for cleaning the windshield.

Be sure to know where to add diesel fuel to the tractor. There is a separate location for adding DEF to the tractor. NEVER add DEF to the diesel tanks. NEVER add diesel fuel to the DEF tank. Always fuel according to the policies and recommendations of the company you drive for and your Driver Manager's recommendations.

If you are pulling a reefer trailer, follow the instructions and recommendations of the company you drive for with regard to where and how to add fuel to the tank of a reefer trailer.

There are also trucks which run on natural gas. These trucks are fueled at the company terminals or at special fuel stations. NEVER add diesel fuel or DEF to the tanks of a natural gas tractor.

All-electric tractors will be as common as diesel trucks one day, and may even be the only Class A Commercial tractors on the road. All-electric tractors will require charging at charge stations to have the necessary power to operate. For more information on all-electric tractors, read chapter 17 - 'Advanced Trucking Technology' and chapter 18 – 'Commercial Electric Vehicles' in this guidebook.

PARKING

Tractor-trailers are large and long vehicles. You can't just park a tractor-trailer anywhere, legally at least. You are required to park at truck stops, company terminals, rest areas, certain shippers (some have parking on their premise), and some weigh stations. Weigh stations which allow parking will usually have a sign that say something like 'PARKING PERMITED AT WEIGH STATION' or 'TRUCK PARKING AT WEIGH STATION'.

Currently, it is illegal to park on exit ramps. I understand the rage of truck drivers. A driver's drive time gets too low, and they have struggled to find parking at truck stops, weigh stations, and other legal locations. That spacious exit ramp will look so enticing in situations like this. Even though DOT or law enforcement might not bother you if you are parked on a ramp, still, park somewhere that is legal. Don't risk getting a citation.

SHOWERS

It's funny when I meet someone who think truck drivers don't shower while away from home. It has happened too often that when I go to shower, any time of the day (sometimes at night), there is a line. One time, at a particular truck stop, there were 12 people waiting in line to get a shower. This was a truck stop which had 15 shower units and all the shower units were occupied, plus the 12 people waiting in line. I also checked in to shower, plus my student at the time, and a married couple walked in after us and requested showers.

Most truck stops have showers. They are cleaned after each use. A towel, small towel, and rag are usually provided. There is usually one soap dispenser in the shower for washing. They have a toilet, counterspace and mirror. I recommend bringing your own rag, towel, and soap just in case the facility you go to shower has none. If you forget, you can ask the facility's staff for a towel and rag.

Showers at truck stops cost money, but big-name truck stop companies have reward programs where you get a free shower every time you fuel a certain minimal gallons of fuel. After you fuel at the same brand name so many gallons, you will eventually earn unlimited free showers. Of course, you have to keep fueling at the same brand to maintain those free showers.

It's refreshing to get a shower at the end of a long driving day, grab some food and head back to the truck and play some tunes or talk with family on the phone while going for a walk!

FOOD

Speaking of food, all truck stops have 'food'. Your common non-perishable snacks and gas station items will be in abundance. Big-name truck stops will usually have hot food of some sorts. Hot dogs, hamburgers, meat rollers, chicken wings, and pizza are common. Big name truck stops usually have fast food restaurants attached such as McDonalds, Burger King, Arby's, and Wendy's.

But there are truck stops I enjoy visiting the most. They are the mom and pop, and family-owned truck stops. They usually have parking when the big-name truck stops are full. They also usually have hot food that is homecooked style and carry hot food that the big names don't. I have eaten some really great meals at these.

Most truck stops also have a small deli section where you will find cold sandwiches, milk, yogurt, cheese, ham, salads, fruit, and other deli foods. You can pretty much formulate an entire diet from food purchased at truck stops. There is food out here for everyone, whatever you eat!

If you are driving a sleeper cab truck, it is likely the truck has a mini fridge and area to place a microwave or air fryer. There is usually an inverter on the truck somewhere as well that power 120v outlets. You can power the air fryer or microwave with this. The sleeper cabs also have plenty of storage underneath the bottom bunk for storing dry and non-perishable foods, and even cases of water. Be sure to measure the microwave area first before buying a microwave or air fryer to ensure it will fit.

Personally, I have a mini fridge (came with the truck), air fryer, hot plate, rice cooker, small stainless pot, and a stainless bowl. It all fits and is hidden so the truck remain spacious inside. All that is seen is the fridge on the passenger side and the air fryer up top. I have literally cooked full course meals from scratch with this setup! It's important for me while I am out on the road weeks at a time!

ENTERTAINMENT

I remember bobtailing to a big-name truck stop one night. I parked where the other bobtails were. After getting out the tractor to head inside to grab some food, I heard what sounded like a movie playing. One of the bobtails had the windows down, and there was a large tv inside which displayed a movie playing on screen. The audio was loud enough to hear outside the truck. It was cold that night and most of the bobtails were not idling their engines. It was entertaining for me to see such a thing. Basically, the inside of the truck was turned into a bedroom/movie theatre!

Some truck companies will allow their drivers to take pets with them while they are out on the road. Each company has their own policy. You will see some drivers with dogs. Although I have never seen any cats (I guess for good reason) or other animals.

Truck companies will usually allow you to bring a family member or friend with you. Be sure to ask your Driver Manager what the policies are for having pets and anyone else onboard.

I have seen other trucks which have gaming systems set up inside so video games can be played when they are not driving. Other drivers will walk around and talk all night on the phone. Some drivers play on their phone when not driving. Others just sit and watch other drivers alley dock into parking spaces! Ha! Some truck stops also have slot machines and other arcade games inside. Everyone has their own entertainment.

Me personally, I enjoy going for short walks, drawing pictures, making phone calls, taking pictures, writing on my laptop, reading, and playing my favorite childhood card game.

SLEEP AND EXERCISE

Driving long hours, hopping in and out the truck several times a day, chatting away on the phone, driving rough roads, and sometimes dealing with angry drivers or pedestrians can exhaust you. Thankfully many tractors are designed as sleeper cabs. They have a bed in the back with a comfortable mattress. Many of these sleeper cab tractors will have double bunks for having two drivers onboard (team driving) and for driver trainers to mentor new drivers. They both will have their own mattress to sleep on and space to place personal items.

Exercise can be difficult due to the long hours driving. But some truck stops have gyms. Rest areas usually have plenty of sidewalks and space to go on a quick stroll. Some truck drivers bring jump ropes or weighted plates with them and exercise while they are not driving. But simply going for a walk at least once a day (no, not to the store to get food!) can help relieve back pain and tension built up in the body from sitting in the hot seat all day.

WEIGH STATIONS/DOT INSPECTIONS

Weigh stations are places which weigh trucks as they pass. If your truck is overweight, or one or more of the axles are overweight, you will be called into the weigh station. There are signs on the road (some that light up) that will tell you if you can pass the weigh station, or if you will need to pull in and get weighed.

The signs may say if the weigh station is open or closed. Most trucks will have some sort of electronic device which will tell you whether you need to pull in or if you can pass the weigh station. Some weigh stations will require you to pull in regardless. Always pay attention to the road signs and the electronic device in the truck you are driving.

If you are overweight on one or more of the axles, the weigh station will require you to slide the tandems and/or 5th wheel until the truck is within legal weight limits. If the cumulative weight is over 80,000 pounds, you will need to follow the instructions given by the DOT officer.

DOT Inspections happen. The DOT officers mean no harm and they perform these inspections for your safety and the safety of others on the road. It is part of their job. Always follow the instructions of all DOT officers and law enforcement. If you are pulled over, don't forget to park, and log 'On-Duty' + 'DOT Inspection' on the ELD.

SCENERY

As you drive, you will certainly visit new places that will be different than where you have lived. It could be the tall mountains and deep canyons, the flying skyscrapers of big cities, cattle filled hills of grass farms, glittering oceans and rivers, or the historic small towns that leave a mysterious pull to your energy. There is a lot to see out there in the world, more than you could ever imagine. Those are just the obvious!

PROMOTIONS – THE PUSH

As you drive and learn the industry, you will be bombarded with opportunities to work for truck companies, become a team driver, move up as a driver trainer or owner operator, and feel the push to keep trucks moving. You may also desire to open your own truck company due to the high amount of work that is out there and the profit that can be made.

The trucking industry is alive, and it will never slow down or take a break. There will always be a load or something that need to be picked up and moved. It won't be long before people and resources will need to be transported back and forth between planets! That will require more than just a couple trucks and a CDL! Ha!

SECTION SIXTEEN
The Trucker Courtesy

As professional truck drivers, it is important we go about our duties in a safe, timely, and courteous manner. Below are some things to take in consideration.

Throw trash into a trash can or dumpster and not on the ground. It is a must to keep clean truck stops, rest areas, weigh stations, and wherever you park. If you want clean facilities, you must take part in helping to keep them clean and free of trash on the ground.

While driving on the Interstate at night, you may find other tractor-trailers flash their headlights after you have passed them and attempt to change back into the right lane. No, they are not angry at you. No, it's not a 'flick them off' gesture! This gesture mean 'safe to switch lanes'. Remember, tractor-trailers are very long vehicles.

While looking in the mirror at the trailer, the trailer looks very short while driving forward. Hours and hours of driving like this can trick the mind into thinking the trailer is actually that short. So, once you have enough space to change lanes over, the driver behind will flash their headlights to signal it is safe to get over.

NEVER assume you always have enough space. Still check the mirrors. After getting back in the right lane, flash your hazard lights to signal 'thank you'. When other tractor-trailer drivers pass you and signal to change back in the right lane, only flash your headlights when it is safe for them to change lanes. Ensure you will have sufficient following distance when they get over.

Never park crooked. If you park crooked, it can make it difficult or impossible for another truck to park in the empty parking space next to you. This could also cause another driver to collide into your tractor or trailer if they attempt to park next to you. Always leave space for traffic flow and other trucks to park. Never block the road, entrance, or exit to any truck stops or facilities. Park in one parking space; don't take up two or multiple parking spaces (unless you are pulling an oversized load). Park within the parking space in a parallel fashion.

Don't block the fuel isle; other trucks need to fuel as well. If you need to fuel, wait in your truck until the truck ahead pull forward, so that you can pull forward in line. If you leave your truck blocking the fuel isle unattended, it will risk being towed or you might get a ticket from a DOT or law enforcement officer.

After you finish fueling, pull up to the line (usually red, white, or yellow) and then park to go inside the store. You must switch to 'Driving' on the ELD when you pull forward. Never idle the engine below 5 mph with the intent to not trip the ELD into the 'Driving' statues.

OTHER THINGS TO CONSIDER

- Don't block other parked trucks. When someone need to leave a parking space, they will need space ahead of them to pull out of the parking space before they can turn. If your tractor and/or trailer is blocking the way for trucks to leave the parking spaces, that could be a big problem.

- Shower time limit – shower when you are ready, don't hold up the showers by checking into a shower and waiting until the clock nearly run out to get in the shower room.

- Park in a parking spot to take your 30-minute break, not in the fuel isle. Other trucks which need fuel would be blocked if you are parked in the fuel isle for a 30-minute break.

- Be patient when trucks are parking, don't blow the horn or try to rush them to park.
- Slow trucks use right lane, prevent moving roadblocks.
- Let truck stop staff know if a fuel pump is not working so they can block it off and call it in for repair.
- Turn on hazard lights while using weigh scale, turn them off when finished and driving off the scale.
- Use the bottom bunk (and not the top bunk) while your teammate, student, or mentor is driving if you need to sleep or lay down. Use the straps or net that is designed with the bottom bunk.

SECTION SEVENTEEN
Advanced Trucking Technology

LEGAL DISCLAIMER: "I do not claim ownership, invention, intellectual property, or patents for any of the technologies mentioned in this chapter. I do not receive funding or payment for mentioning these technologies."

Tractor-trailers have come a long way in new technologies which benefit the drivers and truck companies. Here are some advanced trucking technologies which may soon find their way in the trucks you drive.

- Dashboard embedded ELD (touchscreen) with a preprogrammed CAT Scale app and network updated navigation.

- Electric trailers – solar panels on the roof which charge a small battery pack located at the front of the trailer on the inside. The trailer battery pack charge the electric tractor when hooked with a 'charge cable'. The solar panels charge the small battery pack in the daytime while the trailer is sitting alone with no tractor hooked. The solar panels also charge the tractor's batteries when a tractor is hooked to the trailer. Electric trailers also have a timed light switch which allow checking of the trailer's lights when no tractor is hooked.

- Built-in navigation mimic the voice of loved ones. Several voices can be saved and changed whenever the tractor is in neutral, and the parking brake is set.

- Dashboard embedded magnetic charge pad for a mobile phone. The magnetic charge pad charge a mobile phone wirelessly, and the phone stays to the pad without clips, but with an embedded magnet.

- Air/electric actuated landing gear – the landing gear can be raised or lowered using an electric button or switch located in the cab of the tractor. The landing gear will have geared teeth to prevent the landing gear from raising while the trailer is not hooked to a tractor.
- Trailers with reverse lights, white and bright!
- Variable speed limiter for company trucks (70 mph max in USA). The speed limiter change depending on the speed limit on the interstate the truck is on. The speed limiter is set to 65 while driving on non-interstate roads and highways. The truck will slow down automatically (no brakes applied) if the speed limit lowers, but if the speed limit increases, the driver has to manually accelerate up to a higher speed.
- All new trailers with cab actuated tandem release pins.

SECTION EIGHTEEN
Commercial Electric Vehicles (CEVs)

LEGAL DISCLAIMER: "I do not claim ownership, invention, intellectual property, or patents for anything related to commercial electric vehicles. I do not receive funding or payment for mentioning these technologies."

The time is here that all-electric vehicles are now on our roads and highways. But a different kind of all-electric vehicle will become common place. That is the Commercial Electric Vehicle, also known as the CEV.

There are already many companies and corporations working together to fund the development and sale of all-electric trucks. CEVs will not run on diesel, but purely from electricity stored in battery packs. The CEVs will need to be charged at charging stations. The also will require a new generation of technicians to repair them.

What is interesting is that our current, diesel powered CMVs (Commercial Motor Vehicles), transport the raw materials, products, and parts to make CEVs. But eventually, the CMV will be phased out of the transportation system.

Truck stops may also look different, as they will need to be constructed (or reconstructed) to support the massive charging network needed to keep all the CEVs charged.

As CEV technology improve, and companies employ them on our roads and highways, the trucking industry, and our world as we know it, will change in profound ways.

SECTION NINETEEN
Industry Changes

If someone interviewed me and asked what changes I think would positively impact the trucking industry, the companies, and drivers, I know exactly what I would say. Below are the very things I would tell the interviewer.

LEGAL DISCLAIMER: "I do not claim ownership, invention, intellectual property, or patents for anything related to the changes mentioned below. I do not receive funding or payment for mentioning the technologies and changes mentioned below. These recommended changes are not intended to replace any law, regulations, or instruction given by DOT and law enforcement officers. The recommended changes are not intended to cause any damage, collision, or harm to any vehicles, objects, buildings, persons, or animals. The author and Johnson Craftworks LLC relinquish liability."

1. The first thing I would say is that it would be mandatory all truck schools teach the pull-through, U-turn, straight-line back, and alley-dock. I see these particular maneuvers as essential for all tractor-trailer drivers to be able to perform well without collisions and without damaging the tractor-trailer in any way. The truck schools would also be required to exclude parallel parking. If one can perform the above maneuvers well, the trailer control it take will transfer over to parallel parking.

2. Paid-parking illegal to sell unless the entity/company facilities have showers, hot food, a clocked janitorial rotation, and 24/7 security (manned or electronic). There has been a few times when I have parked at a location in which parking is

FREE, but people came and knocked on my door asking for money to park. It turned out they did not own or work at the facility and were attempting to free-load money. Other times I have parked at paid-only locations and found that the store owners did not pay taxes on the funds from selling paid-parking, and their facilities commonly had dirty bathrooms, no showers, and no hot food. If a driver has to pay for parking. they should get their money's worth.

3. Automatic payout of detention pay from shippers and receivers [to truck companies (or owner operator)] when live load/unload time exceed two hours.

4. Automatic payout of detention pay from shippers and receivers [to truck companies (or owner operator)] when a driver is waiting on a dock drop load/unload and their wait time exceed two hours.

5. Automatic detention pay to company drivers (from the company they drive for) when wait time pass two hours when getting live loaded/unloaded, or waiting on a drop load/unload to finish.

6. All company tractors have speed limiters set to the same speed limit (70 mph). Read chapter 17 of this guidebook for more information on variable speed limiters. I find that speed limiters are a common cause of vehicle collisions and incidents due to the constant lane changes due to tractors having the speed limiters set at different speeds. More lane changes from cars and trucks = more incidents and collisions on the highway. If all company trucks had speed limiters set to the same speed, there would be fewer lane changes, and therefore fewer collisions and incidents.

7. Prohibit zip code to zip code pay by truck companies and fleets (and replace with pay by the mile).

8. Shippers and receivers required to clean trash and debris out of trailers after they unload the trailer or provide a location on site for drivers to sweep out their trailers at no cost to the driver.

9. Shippers and receivers required to have functioning (and accurate) weigh scale on site, follow a maximum load weigh limit law (ex. trailer can be no more than 42,000 pounds loaded), or responsible for paying ticket if an overweight citation is issued to a driver which they loaded. Drivers are still required to weigh the load after getting loaded or hooking to a preloaded trailer to ensure none of the axles exceed the maximum legal limits.

10. Illegal for truck companies to advertise pay and salaries that are for team drivers (and driver trainers) as if they are for solo drivers. Advertisements for solo driver positions and their pay must be and descripted as solo driver pay.

Conclusion

Driving tractor-trailers – not just a job, but an experience. No industry is perfect, the trucking industry has its problems just like any other. But we, together, can make positive changes. It start with facing our fears, challenging ourselves to perform at a higher standard, maintaining a sense of courtesy, and generosity with each other.

I hope that this guidebook has helped you in the way that benefit you the most. Keep it with you, there will always be a use for it. And even if you outgrow it, you have the option to pass it on to someone who wish to become a tractor-trailer driver, or one who already drive, but could benefit from it in some way.

If you wish to contact me, follow me on my social media accounts, or go onto my website, please look at the next page of this guidebook.

Thank you and safe travels!

~ Mr. J

ACKNOWLEDGEMENTS

I want to thank all of my school instructors, driver mentor, students, and all those who helped me along the way. I want to thank all truck drivers for helping to move the world forward.

REVIEW THIS BOOK

Thank you for purchasing this guidebook! Please review and rate this book wherever you purchased it. If the library, website, or eBook provider does not have a rating or review system, use the online Amazon bookstore, Apple Books, or Google Play Books.

Reviews and ratings help drive consumer feedback, book sales, and support for future book ideas.

A three-sentence or single paragraph review along with a 5-STAR ★★★★★ rating is highly recommended and preferred! Thank you for the support and feedback!

BUY ME A COFFEE

BUY ME A COFFEE, TEA, OR COCONUT WATER!
THANK YOU!

BITCOIN (BTC) ADDRESS:
bc1qv3uxjj57d05gymkaz2y2nwnl4ej3vkxtn4a295

Please mention this guidebook's name, The Johnson Method, in the note or comments section when sending Bitcoin or purchasing item off my wish list

AMAZON WISH LIST:

*By sending BTC Bitcoin or purchasing item(s) from the wish list, you agree to the disclaimer written below.

LEGAL DISCLAIMER: "The author and Johnson Craftworks LLC are not liable for BTC Bitcoin sent to the wrong address or person. Sending BTC Bitcoin to the above address may incur a fee (transfer, processing, international, transaction, or conversion). Cash, debit/credit card, check, wire transfer, ACH/checking, money, fiat currencies, and NFTs are not accepted. BTC Bitcoin sent ARE NON-REFUNDABLE. Johnson Craftworks LLC and the author do not send any communications (or requests) asking for cryptocurrency, NFTs, payment, debt collection, or repayment.

Terrence Johnson accepts BTC Bitcoin and items purchased from the above wish list as gifts. Goods, products, and services are not provided for the receiving of BTC Bitcoin and items from the above wish list. Company ownership, shares, and equity are not provided for the receiving of BTC Bitcoin and items from the above wish list

PRODUCT STORE

CLICK HERE TO SHOP 100% NATURAL GEMSTONE TALISMANS, GOLD AND SILVER CUBAN LINK CHAINS, AND GIFTS FOR YOUR SIGNIFICANT OTHER.

SOCIAL MEDIA & CONTACT INFO

EMAIL: contact@johnsoncraftworks.com

YOUTUBE: @newtruckerradio

TIKTOK: @paragonsblaze

RUMBLE: EXCELLENCE on Fire!

INSTAGRAM: @paragonsblaze

By viewing, engaging, subscribing to, messaging, contacting, following, liking, sharing, and commenting on the above email and social media accounts, you agree to the terms and conditions as described on the same email and social media accounts. No adult content allowed. No soliciting. Any names or accounts other than the ones listed above are non-original or are old accounts no longer in use.

LEGAL DISCLAIMER – The website and social media are not created for the purpose of any person, entity, or organization to engage in illegal activities, damage property, defamation of any person, or causing any kind of harm to any person or animal (including themselves). The website and social media are created for enterjoyment, educational, and communication purposes only. Johnson Craftworks LLC and Terrence Johnson relinquish liability.

OTHER BOOKS BY AUTHOR

Have you ever wondered why you keep attracting NARCS or the same type of lovers? Do you wonder why no matter what you do, you just can't seem to get him (or her) to love you or behave better? Do your lovers cheat on you or run from you, keeping you at arms distance?

In this guidebook, you will discover the Mirrored Self, and the Twin Soul. this is a soulful book. It is a knowledgeable, realistic, and spiritual take on the most significant relationship, the one with your Self. All other relationships and connections with other people are a direct mirror of your own soul, and of your Self. Want a better lover and a deeper, more pleasing love? Read on to find out!

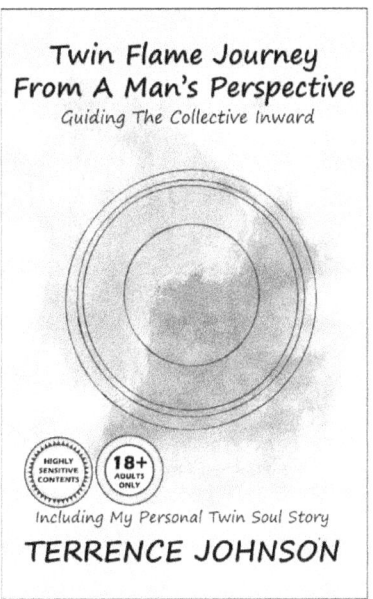

Available on Amazon, Google Play, Apple Books and more!

Johnson Craftworks LLC
Copyright © 2023
All Rights Reserved
United States of America

www.ingramcontent.com/pod-product-compliance
Lightning Source LLC
Chambersburg PA
CBHW050641160426
43194CB00010B/1759